Beyond Belief

Books by Edward W. Bauman
Published by The Westminster Press ®

Beyond Belief

An Introduction to the New Testament

The Life and Teaching of Jesus

Intercessory Prayer

Beyond Belief

by

EDWARD W. BAUMAN

THE WESTMINSTER PRESS

Philadelphia

LIBRARY OF CONGRESS CATALOG CARD No. 64–14088

Published by The Westminster Press ®
Philadelphia, Pennsylvania 19107

PRINTED IN THE UNITED STATES OF AMERICA

FOR AUDREE
Comrade in Every Adventure

CONTENTS

PREFACE

I N THE ROLLING HILLS of central Ohio there is a farm-
house built around an ever-flowing spring of pure
water. The original owners, welcoming the discovery of the
spring as a good omen, first enclosed it in a little spring room
and then literally built the house around it. For nearly half a
century now, day and night, that steady stream of clear water
has been flowing out of the earth into the spring room, bringing
strength and refreshment to all who live in the house around it.

In just this same way it is possible for human beings to build
their lives around a spring of living water flowing out of a
center deep within. Jesus spoke to the woman at Jacob's Well
about this astounding possibility. "Whoever drinks of the water
that I shall give him," said Jesus, "will never thirst; the water
that I shall give him will become in him a spring of water
welling up to eternal life." This spring of water welling up to
eternal life is the Spirit of God within us, the living presence of
God, who is the Ground of all being. Deep within every man
this spring wells up to offer us fullness of life. God has created
us so that we are restless and uncertain, houses divided against
ourselves, until we discover and build around this inner source
of our true existence.

This book is about the one thing needful in human life, the
discovery and acceptance of the creative life made possible by

this inner spring of living water, the Spirit of God within us. In this creative life, now made available to all men through Jesus Christ, man realizes the basic purpose for his existence. We will be especially concerned with basic Christian belief about this creative life in Christ, particularly in view of the present theological revolution in words and ideas. But we will also be aware of the sheer wonder of a God who comes to us in this living way and of the creative possibilities in the new life made possible by his coming. It is, in short, the story of a faith that is at the same time thoroughly believable and utterly beyond belief.

E. W. B.

Washington, D.C.

PROLOGUE

Christian Life

I s THE CHRISTIAN FAITH RELEVANT in a twentieth-century world that has intellectually come of age? Does the Christian gospel still provide the most meaningful answer to the problem of human existence? Is authentic Christian life possible in the modern world and is it psychologically healthful?

Many influential persons, convinced that we have moved into a post-Christian era, are answering these vital questions with a resounding "No!" Christian belief, we are told, is not only outmoded but positively harmful, stunting man's natural development and robbing him of the freedom to pursue his highest destiny. This view is proclaimed as "gospel" not only on college campuses but in living rooms and church discussion groups, in cocktail lounges and coffeehouses. The general feeling is that we must look beyond Christianity to more exciting things because the Christian religion "simply has not kept up with the times."

Part of the problem may be attributed to modern man's insistence on intellectual integrity and his naïve assumption that Christian faith is unreasonable and unbelievable. How can we hold to the Biblical view of creation when science has demonstrated the truth of evolution? How can we accept the idea of original sin when psychology and sociology provide other ex-

11

planations for our human predicament? Who can make any
sense out of a blood atonement or a God who becomes flesh
and dies? Why do Christians continue to talk about a God "up
there" or "out there" when everyone knows God is neither up
nor out anywhere? Such questions often imply that it is necessary
to crucify the intellect in order to become a faithful Christian!

There is a delightful story about Groucho Marx and the
Friars Club, an exclusive organization of actors and show people.
As a member, Groucho was attending the annual banquet and
listening to a famous speaker deliver an address on the subject
"The Show Must Go On!" This old cliché was repeated over
and over until Groucho could stand it no longer. He stood up
and shouted, "Why?" This flustered the speaker so much he
couldn't continue because he had never really considered why.
The directors of the club angrily tried to expel Groucho, but he
would not let them have the last word. He outmaneuvered them
by sending in a letter of resignation, stating that he refused to
be a member of a club "low down enough" to accept him for
membership in the first place.

Still the question lingers. "Why?" When Christian ministers
and teachers endlessly repeat the old religious clichés, increasing
numbers of persons are tempted to stand up and shout, "Why?"
Unfortunately, many well-meaning Christians respond to the
challenge of this question by retreating into deeper obscurity.
They speak very knowingly of "mystery" and "paradox," devel-
oping a special vocabulary for the exclusive use of the ingroup.
Voices out of the past are quoted, from Tertullian to Kierkegaard, condemning "that harlot reason." Departments of religion
in many colleges refuse to enter into the rough-and-tumble of
dialogue with other departments because the truths of Christianity are "revealed" and are therefore not subject to confrontation by opposing views. There is also more than a little
significance in the growing popularity of "speaking in tongues."
This practice may or may not be a valid expression of Christian

experience, but as far as the world at large is concerned, it is the last straw. As one professor remarked to me, "This phenomenon is the climax of the Christian 'babbling' which has been getting more irrelevant and unbelievable all the time."

What this professor and others have missed is the significant activity among dedicated Christian scholars, who are demonstrating that the Christian faith is intellectually respectable and appealing. They admit that the basic truths have come down to us dressed in mythological forms largely unacceptable to modern man, but this does not mean that the essential core of Christian truth must be discarded. On the contrary, after a process of demythologizing, the essence of Christianity is found to be more relevant and meaningful than ever before. It may still contain the intellectual "scandal" of the cross at the center, but this is not at all unbelievable in the way ancient myths and thought forms are unbelievable. The problem is to describe and communicate the essential core of Christian faith without straining the integrity of modern man by depending on traditional words and thought patterns.

It is highly significant that Rudolf Bultmann, the foremost demythologizer, was originally motivated by the desire to shear away the unintelligible jargon of Christian dogma and present the gospel in its profound simplicity to simple laboring folk. Similarly, Dietrich Bonhoeffer's thought was deeply influenced by the practical difficulties he encountered in communicating the gospel to soldiers at the front during the Second World War. During the last days of his life he wrote from the concentration camp about the need in this twentieth century for "Christianity without religion." By this he simply meant Christian faith freed from the crumbling old wineskins no longer capable of holding the bubbling new wine of the Spirit. More familiar, perhaps, to Americans is the work of Paul Tillich. How can we account for the popularity of a man whose sentence structure is often complicated and whose ideas are so weighty? Countless persons confess that he speaks to their deepest needs because of the way he transforms traditional religious symbolism into contemporary terms. He is a bridge-builder, in the best sense of that word, from within the theological circle to modern man in his "existential predicament."

The work of Bultmann, Bonhoeffer, and Tillich is typical of theology's present concern with interpreting the essence of Christian faith to men of our time. Vitally important as this work is, however, there are still countless persons who have not been touched by it to any large degree. For several years I have been conducting a class in religion over a commercial television station. The thousands of letters we have received reveal the urgent need for continuing attempts to state the essence of Christian faith in direct, intelligible terms. One man spoke in a colorful way for most of the others when he wrote to me, "Cut out all the theological frills and give me the guts of religion so that I can believe!"

Forced to face this kind of question in my correspondence and in preparation for the weekly television program, I found myself constantly struggling to find the most effective method of presenting the Christian gospel to our modern world. I discovered that what the minister or teacher says and what his listeners actually "hear" are often worlds apart. Time and time again I asked the question, "Have I really said this in the most direct and relevant way?" What about the salesmen who are listening, the prisoners, the firemen, the housewives, the young people? In addition to all this, I began to work one night a week in the coffeehouse that was opened several years ago by the well-known Church of the Saviour in Washington, D. C. Here I found artists, scientists, writers, Government workers, and other business and professional people who were open to the permanent validity of the Christian message when it was presented in an intellectually respectable way. But could I honestly state it in this way? What do you say in those fleeting moments around a coffeehouse table when men and women and young people are truly listening? In those conversations in a coffeehouse I found myself discarding a great deal of excess theological baggage.

This growing need for direct and believable statements of the Christian faith has become an urgent challenge to Christians in contemporary culture. This book is intended to speak to this need, but we must hasten to point out that this is only part of the problem. Ironically, much of the modern theological writing intended to clarify Christian faith has actually complicated the situation by misleading persons into believing that the essence of Christianity is found in believing the right things. We must never minimize the importance of intelligible belief, but nothing could be more harmful than leading people to believe that they will become Christians by straightening out their theological ideas. Yet this is precisely the impression many people are receiving from much contemporary writing and discussion.

A good example is *Honest to God,* the highly controversial book by John A. T. Robinson. This forthright and dedicated Anglican bishop has tried to be "honest to God and honest about God" as he questions many basic assumptions held by Christians in the past. His purpose is in direct accord with those who are eager to communicate the essence of Christian faith to men of our time. The phenomenal popularity of the book is a convincing demonstration of the need for this approach. But after reading the book and talking with others who have read it, I am forced to ask the question, "Is *Honest to God* really honest to God?" Does it communicate the essence of Christian experience? Is this the heart of Christian faith or is something missing? So often the author seems to be playing theological word games and manipulating theological ideas to make them fit contemporary thought forms, leaving the impression that this is all there is to it. We must insist, on the contrary, that correct intellectual belief, important as it is, is not the essence of the Christian life.

There are, in fact, two things about the Christian life that are "beyond belief," not in the sense of being unbelievable but in the sense of being more fundamental. First, beyond the belief of a Christian there is the unique action of God's grace in his life and in the world. The Christian life is not first of all something man believes, but something God initiates and offers to man through his grace. Apart from the prior action of this grace there could be no meaningful belief. Second, beyond the belief of a Christian there is a new fullness of life resulting from his response to God's grace. Correct belief contributes to this fullness of life, but it by no means constitutes the whole.

As far as the first is concerned, anyone reading the New Testament soon discovers that the writers are not primarily interested in conveying beliefs about God and Jesus. This is part of their purpose, of course, but their chief interest is in sharing the good news of something God has done for them and for the world. The God who is the Creator of man has acted graciously as a Redeemer to save man from estrangement and despair. He has not waited for man to take the first step, nor has he waited for man to become worth saving. On the contrary, he has acted in sheer love, taking the initiative, and offering man a new fullness of life. Christians have used the word "grace" to describe this action of God's redemptive love. Grace is the outpouring of love beyond what is expected or deserved. It is the offering of love unconditionally. The early Christians simply couldn't stop talking about how they had experienced this grace of God in Jesus Christ. It wasn't so much a matter of what they believed as it was a matter of *what had happened to them.*

Someone once asked psychologist William James if he believed in infant Baptism. With tongue in cheek, he replied, "Believe in it? Why, man, I've seen it!" The early Christians might well have made a similar reply to anyone who asked them about their belief in Christ. "It is not a matter of believing in him when we have seen him, heard him, and known him in our own experience." We may agree with those who insist that some aspects of the New Testament description of God's "coming" in Christ have become unintelligible. How can we believe in a God "up there" who "breaks into" human history to "become flesh" and reveal his gracious purpose for the world? Such word pictures spoke to the first century but seem strangely inadequate in an age acutely aware of the nature of outer space. Yet the truth symbolized in the words is at the heart of the Christian life because this is precisely the way Christians have experienced God's action in their own lives. We may think of God as beyond or within, we may speak of him as Ultimate Reality, we may refer to him as the Father or Ground of our being. But whatever symbols best suit our contemporary age, the truth is that this God (Ultimate Reality, Father, Ground of our being) acts in our human situation in a gracious, loving, purposive way. It is this act of God, prior to all human belief, that gives man ultimate hope concerning his existence. Too many recent works in theology have failed to emphasize this priority of God's grace as the foundation of all Christian life and belief.

A second aspect of the Christian life is also more fundamental than mere intellectual belief. This is the fullness of life resulting from man's free response to God's grace. Our belief has a direct influence on the way we live, but life is more than belief. Christian life includes the creative surrender of the whole self—mind, body, emotions, will—to God's redemptive grace. This act, freely undertaken by a responsible person, is the only way to the fulfillment of the self. "Believing" in this life is important, but there are many persons who believe these things intellectually, yet utterly fail to exemplify the life they think about and speak about so brilliantly. Indeed, intellectual speculation may become an effective way of escaping the rigors of Christian discipleship. Beyond the most sophisticated belief there always remains the problem of living the full Christian life.

This is what Dietrich Bonhoeffer was talking about in his

striking comparison of cheap grace and costly grace. Cheap grace, he insists, is the deadly enemy of the church. It is grace as a doctrine, a principle, a system. It is forgiveness of sins proclaimed as a general truth without requiring repentance and amendment of life. Costly grace, on the other hand, calls us to leave our nets and follow one who demands everything of us; indeed, this grace costs a man his whole life. But in losing his life in this way, he finds it again, receiving it from God in new form and in new fullness. When Jesus was asked about the signs of true disciple-ship, he did not give any theological principles or creeds, but responded simply, "You will know them by their fruits."

One of the main purposes of this book is to state the essentials of Christian belief in a relevant and intelligible way. But we are insisting that such a discussion will be misleading apart from an emphasis on the totality of Christian experience, especially the grace of God, which makes belief possible, and the fullness of life that results from it. Accordingly, each of the following chapters will be divided into three main parts. The first will emphasize the grace of God as experienced by Christians; the second will describe certain basic areas of Christian belief; the third will point toward the fullness of life made possible by our experience of God's grace and by our belief about it. In this way we will be able to focus on the central problem while maintaining a proper sense of perspective.

There is a great deal of talk these days about how the world has come of age intellectually. This idea challenges every Chris-tian believer to make his faith as intelligible and relevant as pos-sible. It is obvious, however, that in many ways man has hardly come of age at all. Indeed, he is like an infant trembling on the threshold of life, eager to grow but afraid of the unknown. This book is for all those who are facing life in this unknown future. It is a book about a unique faith that is relevant and believable in every age because it is grounded in the good news of a gracious God who offers creative and affirmative fullness of life to all men.

CHAPTER 1

Existence

I GOT SO BORED watching television," said Gian-Carlo Menotti, "that I wrote this little opera as a protest. A PROTEST." In this way one of America's leading composers describes the birth of *Labyrinth,* an opera that turns out to be a protest against more than meaningless television. It is in a much deeper way a protest against meaningless life. The action centers around a newly married couple, wandering in search of their room through the endless corridors of a rambling old hotel. But the search is futile. Even when they find the room, they discover that the door is locked and that they have lost the key.

Modern man, Menotti is saying, has lost the key to the labyrinth of life. As his days run their course, he may become frantic in his search for a way out or he may resign himself to a lifetime of restless wandering. But in either case the future is hopeless because there is no way for man to discern any ultimate meaning or purpose for his existence.

Menotti's solution is death. At the end of the opera, the groom is nailed into a coffin and wakes up in the afterlife holding the lost key. "Death is not the end of life," explains Menotti, "but its very happy solution." But is this really a solution? Must we admit so readily that life before death is empty and futile? Menotti's lost key, Sartre's nothingness, and Camus' absurdity

19

are typical of an often repeated theme in modern thought. Life
in this world is ultimately meaningless.

A. BEYOND BELIEF: GOD'S GRACE

Anyone familiar with the history of man's search for meaning
knows that such laments are not new. Even Ecclesiastes, one of
the books in the Bible, is based on this theme. Written some
two or three centuries before the birth of Christ, Ecclesiastes has
been called the most modern writing in the Old Testament
because of the author's despair over the "lost key" of life. He does
not doubt the existence of God, but he protests bitterly that the
ways of God are unknowable. God has given man a purpose for
his life, but he refuses to reveal what that purpose is. He has
placed a longing for eternity in the heart of man but has shown
him no way to satisfy the longing. We can understand something
about "a time to be born and a time to die," but the time between
is filled with frustrating emptiness because God refuses to reveal
the purpose for existence.

The overwhelming contrast between this "modern" mood and
the rest of the Biblical record is so obvious that even the most
casual reader cannot miss it. Part of the sheer wonder of life,
the other books insist, is that the Holy God has revealed the ultimate purpose for human existence. All would agree that because
God is God, he could choose to remain unknowable, allowing
man to wander in the labyrinth without a key. But he has not
chosen to do so! Instead, God has had a gracious purpose for
human life from the beginning and he has made that purpose
clearly known. God has acted in human history; God has come
to man; God has provided man with the key to life's meaning.

In simplest terms, the Bible is trying to say that human life
has meaning only when we are creatively related to God. This
order of existence has been established by God himself and has
been clearly revealed to men. Human beings have been brought
into existence for this purpose. Until we discover that Ulti-

mate Reality is structured in this way, until we accept this "God fact" for our own lives, we wander hopelessly in deadening circles of futility and fear.

As early as the time of Moses, the Old Testament community showed signs of apprehending this fact about existence. Out of all the people of the earth, they believed God had chosen them to be his own particular people. They described their unique relationship with God as a covenant or binding agreement. The covenant was not something that they invented. On the contrary, it was a gift of God's grace. It was offered to them purely out of God's love for them and for all men. As long as they remained faithful to their covenant with God, life was rich and moved in a purposive direction. But any reader of the Old Testament is familiar with the record of broken covenants, of unfaithfulness, and of growing estrangement between Israel and God. One of the astounding things about human life is that even when we know that the purpose of life is realized in relationship with God, we choose to rebel and try to walk alone. It has been this way from the beginning.

Through this rebellion and its tragic consequences it became increasingly clear that Israel's way of life was doomed to failure because it was contrary to the very "nature of things." As Martin Luther suggested, we might even expect the story to end with God's final rejection of his stubborn children. But still God's grace continued to manifest itself even in Israel's rebellion. If one part of the Old Testament is a record of broken covenants and unfaithfulness, the other is a story of continuing forgiveness and renewal. God continued to call man into relationship with himself even in the face of continuing rejection. To our astonishment the Old Testament ends with a promise that God's purpose will soon be even more clearly revealed in a Messiah, one whose life will be the supreme revelation of what every man's life is intended to be.

This promise was fulfilled in Jesus the Christ. The New Testament cries out in exultant joy that this One who came to live among us is the perfect example of the divine intention for every man. He is "the key" to human life. Man finds his way out of the labyrinth when he follows this path and lives out his days in the way revealed by this Christ. His life is the supreme example of the God-man relationship that gives meaning to every life. Does a man really want to know the purpose for his existence? Then let him enter into the kind of relationship with God that has been revealed in Jesus the Christ.

We will have much more to say about this God-man relationship as the key to human existence. The important thing to note here is that our crucial knowledge about the meaning of life comes as a result of God's initiative. God does not, as Ecclesiastes believed, create man and then leave him to knock about in futility. From the beginning, God has acted in human history to reveal clearly and directly the purpose for human existence. Some theologians do not like to say "God comes to us," because this implies that he has not been "in us" and "with us" all the time. But there is an important truth symbolized in the phrase "comes to us." God's gracious activity in revealing the meaning of life is something that happens to us, something we experience, something that grasps us, something that is freely given to us. It is not first of all something we "believe in," and it is never something we think up or invent. It is the activity of God that "comes to us," "breaks in upon us," and is given to us in our experience. In this sense, it is beyond belief.

B. BASIC BELIEF

It is impossible to enter into many areas of contemporary literature without experiencing both pathos and astonishment. How, for example, can a brilliant writer like Camus conclude that life is ultimately absurd? The real absurdity is that such a man missed the profoundly simple "key" to life's meaning in terms of man's relationship with Ultimate Reality. There are clear indications that Camus caught glimpses of this truth from time to time. Once he wrote of an "invincible summer" he found within himself. But nothing ever came of it, and we wonder why. Where were the Christian voices that could have interpreted this invincible summer to a man of brilliant intellect and sensitive spirit? Could it be that Christians have not spoken clearly about the meaning of life to others because they have not worked it through in their own thinking? What do we believe about the key to life's meaning revealed by God in Jesus Christ?

The confusion arises partly from the fact that several terms are used in the Biblical record to describe Christian belief about man's basic relationship with God. Each term arose out of a particular historical situation, but all refer to the same basic divine-human relationship that is God's intention for every life.

The opening chapter of the Bible states, for example, that man has been created in *the image of God* (Gen. 1:26–27). This phrase is sometimes interpreted to mean that there is something in the nature of man, such as freedom or reason, that makes him like God. But such an approach misses the profound truth in the concept "image of God." The image of God refers to the reflection of God's life in the life of man whenever man stands in a responsive relationship to God. The important thing is not some faculty or capacity in man, but man's position before God, that makes it possible for him to "image" God. It is significant that this phrase is used in the first chapter of Genesis, for it emphasizes man's responsive relationship with his Creator as a divine intention from the beginning. By moving out of his position before God, man distorts the image and thwarts the purpose for his creation.

Another Biblical term used to define the ultimate meaning of human existence has already been mentioned. From earliest times, the people of Israel spoke of God's *covenant* with them. Covenants were of many kinds in the ancient world, but they were usually binding agreements between persons or groups.

God's covenant with Israel was a result of his gracious purpose
for Israel in particular and for human life in general. In offering
the covenant to Israel, God promised that life would be meaningful as long as the people were faithful to the covenant bond. The
most helpful interpreters of the Old Testament in our time have
been emphasizing the centrality of the covenant, not only in the
life of Israel but as the means God chose to reveal his purpose
for all mankind. Isaiah and Jeremiah had both insisted on this
universal meaning of the covenant. Others had expressed the need
for continuing interpretation of the covenant concept, a need
answered by Jesus in the upper room on the last night of his life.
As he shared the bread and wine with his disciples, he referred
to his death as the sealing of the new covenant, a covenant that
was not a rejection of the old but its fulfillment. The purpose
of the old covenant had been to establish an eternal bond between
God and man. Jesus seems to be saying that this purpose is now
fulfilled in his life and in his death. In view of this emphasis, it
is not surprising to find a revival of covenant theology in contemporary religious thought.

Although Jesus referred to the covenant in this basic way, other
phrases were even more often on his lips. In the first three
Gospels the theme of his teaching is the *Kingdom of God*. The
purpose of his first sermon, reported by Mark, was to announce
that the Kingdom is at hand. From this time on, the phrase was
constantly in his preaching and teaching. Most of the parables
begin, "The kingdom of God is like. . . ." Sometimes he talked
about man and the Kingdom, sometimes about himself and the
Kingdom, more often about God and the Kingdom, but the
Kingdom is always the common point of reference. In spite of the
excitement caused by his power to heal, he never let this phase
of his ministry interfere with the proclamation of the Kingdom.
On the contrary, he said that the healing was simply a sign that
the Kingdom had come. He taught his disciples to pray for the
Kingdom, he told them to seek first the Kingdom, and he did

this himself in every incident of his life and in every word of his teaching.

But what is the Kingdom of God in the teaching of Jesus? Unfortunately, modern readers often miss the principal idea conveyed by the phrase in the New Testament. The Kingdom of God means primarily the kingly "rule" or "reign" of God. Many modern versions of the New Testament translate the Greek words in this way, thus capturing the intended idea of relationship between king and subject. A person enters the Kingdom of God when he freely accepts the total rule of the King in every area of his life. He allows God's ruling activity to guide and shape every aspect of his being. The idea of entering the Kingdom does not mean losing one's individuality in a group of persons who are blindly obedient to an autocratic ruler. It means, on the contrary, entering a community of love made up of those who have joyfully accepted God's total rule in their lives, thus fulfilling the primary purpose for their existence.

In John's Gospel the phrase *eternal life* is often used by Jesus to refer to the same divine-human relationship. Jesus defined it quite clearly in his prayer in the upper room: "This is eternal life, that they know thee the only true God, and Jesus Christ whom thou has sent" (John 17:3). This "knowing" God is not merely knowing about him, but knowing him through the deepest involvement of the whole person with God. The most creative bond between persons comes into being as husband and wife "know" one another at the deepest levels of life-sharing. In the Bible the same word is often used to refer to the bond between husband and wife and to the bond between God and man. Entering into this knowing relationship with God is entering eternal life.

It is unfortunate that many persons think of eternal life only as a future life that begins after death and continues into eternity. In this way of thinking, man's present life becomes primarily preparation for an eternal future state of joy or sorrow. But the meaning that Jesus conveyed is much more deeply rooted in man's present existence. When he spoke of eternal life he was referring to a present quality of life, to the reality of life as it can be known here and now. Eternal life is thus not a reward for virtue; it is the virtuous life itself. It is unconditional love of God now, joyful obedience to him now, fulfilling fellowship with him now as well as forever. "All the way to heaven is heaven!"

The apostle Paul speaks of both the Kingdom of God and eternal life, but he also uses the phrase *life in Christ*. This had particular meaning for him because of the way in which he became one with God through Jesus Christ. Prior to his conversion, Paul had been eagerly seeking to relate himself to God, but he was going about it in the wrong way. Through Christ he discovered the way of true reconciliation with God, and his life was so changed that he literally felt that he had become a new being. Because all this happened to him through Christ, he often spoke of his new life "in Christ." Albert Schweitzer and others have pointed out the deep, mystical overtones in the phrase "in Christ," but this need not distract those who cannot, like Paul, be caught up in experiences of mystical ecstasy. Paul is primarily communicating in this way something of the new relationship with God found through Christ, a relationship in which he finally realized the purpose for his own existence.

Image of God, covenant, Kingdom of God, eternal life, life in Christ—all these phrases will take on richer meaning as they are related to ideas and experiences yet to be described. The essential thing to note at this point is the common core of meaning. In speaking of our basic belief about the meaning of human existence, we may say that we believe man is created in the image of God. We may say we believe in the covenant bond between God and man. We may speak of our belief in the Kingdom of God or eternal life as the one thing needful. We may refer to our new life in Christ. But in each case we are pointing toward our basic belief that man has been created for God. Human life is so constituted that we never come to the fullest realization of the self until we have entered into the deepest relationship with God.

Here, then, is the key to the labyrinth of human existence. It is not a key man has devised, not a scheme man has invented. It is a key provided by God. At a later point we will face the problem of finding the most helpful way of referring to the God who has provided this key. Some persons find it meaningful to think of him as a loving Father, others as the Ground of being. But the essential truth remains. As finite beings, we fulfill the purpose for our existence only through responsive relationship with the God who is our Father and the Ground of all being.

C. Beyond Belief: Fullness of Life

One basic truth about the Christian life is so obvious that it is often overlooked by those who talk and write about it most. This is the simple fact that Christian belief is not really *Christian* belief unless it leads to Christian life. Here is a faith to be lived every moment by the whole person, a faith to be enjoyed to the fullest, a faith to be experienced in each present moment of existence. One reason why thoughtful persons such as Albert Camus have rejected the Christian "key" to existence is that they have not seen it demonstrated in the lives of Christian people. Following the leadings of his inquiring mind, Camus often participated in lengthy discussions on the problems of Christian belief. But he was discouraged by the fact that the Christians he knew were, in the long run, like everyone else. Their belief made no difference in the handling of real life, or what is worse, it often made them gloomy and negative about those things in life which demanded joy and affirmation.

Why is it that professing Christians so often break down at the point of actualizing their faith in life? Jesus seemed to be aware of the problem, for he spoke a great deal about the importance of "bearing fruit" and actually "doing the will" of the Father. The best-known single collection of his teachings, the Sermon on the Mount, is primarily a picture of how a Christian lives, not what he believes. It ends with three unforgettable parables—the two ways, the two trees, the two houses—and in each case the emphasis is on those who hear *and do* the will of God.

Blessed is the man who has discovered the fullness of life that grows out of the basic belief described in such terms as "Kingdom of God" or "eternal life." He is a man who has found a creative sense of direction for his essential being. He moves with quiet certainty and with great effectiveness because he knows where he is going. Having found the open road, he no longer has to expend great amounts of energy exploring dead-end streets and endlessly retracing his steps. There are times of darkness, of course, for no one escapes physical and mental suffering. But there is a vast difference between the sufferer who can relate his suffering to some deeper purpose and the one who is helplessly caught in the tides of chance and misfortune. This creative sense of direction is one of the manifestations of the full life that is rooted and grounded in God.

Another is the feeling of coherence about life. Many persons complain about the broken and diffused nature of experience. There are too many things demanding our attention, too many aspects of consciousness that are not related. In one of Tennessee Williams' plays a mentally ill woman spends countless hours seated in a garden trying to put a jigsaw puzzle together. Every now and then she looks up with panic in her eyes and cries out pathetically: "The pieces don't fit together! The pieces don't fit together!" We often feel this way about life until we find the central piece that supplies the key to the entire puzzle. Once this piece is discovered, all the other pieces fall into place around it.

In more practical terms, what we are trying to say is that the person who has discovered the basic meaning of existence experiences a wholeness about life that comes in no other way.

There is a positive and healthful attitude of self-acceptance that leads to a positive and healthful attitude toward others. Dynamic psychology has been emphasizing this need for direction and wholeness if the individual is to possess mental well-being. Dr. Viktor E. Frankl, a prominent psychiatrist, spent a lengthy period of time in a concentration camp during the Second World War. He observed that the majority of individuals with the stamina and courage to struggle for survival were those who had found some basic purpose for living. Others simply gave up. He was so impressed with this fact that he founded a school of psychiatry based on this fundamental human need for meaning and purpose.

It is a dazzling experience to approach the Christian faith for the first time and see the possibility of rich and radiant life opening up in all directions. It is even more astounding to discover that this type of existence is freely offered by a gracious God to all men. It soon becomes apparent, however, that the offer is not forced upon us. We must seek the gift and ask for it and knock on the door behind which it rests. We must accept it through discipline and obedience and costly discipleship. There are few who will pay this price. Few are willing to make the effort to move into creative fullness of life. But the mystery of why so many reject the one thing in life that is truly needful leads us now to the fundamental problem of sin and estrangement.

CHAPTER 2

Estrangement

THERE APPEARED on Broadway many years ago an intriguing drama called *The Man Who Played God*. The title referred to a deaf man who lived in an apartment high above Central Park in New York City. Using powerful binoculars, he read the lips of people seated on park benches far below. To those in trouble he sent a servant with word that help was on the way. When asked the source of this help, the servant replied, "It comes from the man who plays God."

This haunting line is actually a reflection of the most tragic fact in human life, the desire of every man to play God. In the Broadway play it resulted in benevolent attitudes toward others. But in real life it inevitably causes us to harm others and destroy ourselves. We have seen how all men are created for meaningful relationship with God. But only God is God. Human beings are finite and totally dependent upon him. Yet we refuse to acknowledge this fact of our human condition. We will not accept our limited, finite, and dependent state. On the contrary, we try to play God with our own lives and with the lives of others. The result is estrangement from the one true God and a life of constant frustration and despair. In attempting to escape from this situation, we either collapse and "break down" completely, or we assert autonomy even more aggressively, thus ending in deeper despair. Who can deliver us from this tragic predicament?

30

A. Beyond Belief: God's Grace

One of the most remarkable aspects of human existence is the fact of individual freedom. "Man has been created free, and is free, even in chains." Because of this freedom, we may choose to accept or reject fellowship with God and thus determine our ultimate destiny as persons. God creates us. God reveals himself to us. God calls us to himself. But the choice is always ours. Otherwise, it would be meaningless to speak of creative relationship between man and God.

Those who have experienced the overwhelming power of God's being in the depths of their own being occasionally overlook the significance of human freedom. John Calvin is often attacked at this point because he developed a doctrine of predestination that seems to deny individual freedom of choice. This doctrine grew out of his profound awareness of the sovereign majesty of a God who alone is responsible for the creation and salvation of men. Yet even Calvin recognized that the complete denial of freedom was a denial of the deepest meaning of the divine salvation that he was trying to defend. In attacking some of his enemies, Calvin wrote: "They attribute to man no free will, any more than if he were a stone; and they remove all distinction between good and evil so that nothing can be done wrongly, in their opinion, since God is the author of it. . . . Dreadful consequences follow."

The most dreadful consequence, it is easy to see, is the destruction of the dynamic bond between God and man that is the ground of meaningful human existence. For such a bond to have meaning, man must have the power of contrary choice, the ability to determine the direction of his own destiny. In view of current world affairs, it is ironical to discover many Russian writers, such as Berdyaev, Dostoevsky, Tolstoy, and Pasternak, expressing themselves on this subject with telling effect.

To cite one example, Tolstoy's description of the death of Ivan Ilyitch is one of the most moving in all literature. It is the story of a man who suffers indescribable mental and physical pain in his dying hours. He cries out for death to come and relieve his agony, yet he is terrified at the thought of death. He longs for human love and understanding, but he cannot stand to have people watch him suffer. And then the screaming began, screaming that continued for three days "and was so terrible that one could not hear it through two closed doors without horror. . . . He struggled as a man condemned to death struggles in the hands of the executioner, knowing that he cannot save himself." The turning point came when Ivan discovered even in the midst of his agony an area of freedom. He was not free to stop the suffering, but he was free to decide what to make of it. He was free to think about what his suffering could mean to other people. Above all, he was free to admit at last that his life had not been what it should have been and he was free to repent. The discovery and use of his freedom in these last moments made such a difference that the man who had been screaming in pain for three days died quietly, and his last audible words expressed his feeling at having discovered meaning in the midst of pain. "So that's what it is!" he suddenly exclaimed aloud. "What joy!"

What joy to experience freedom as a gift of God, a gift that makes possible the actual choice of creative values in each moment of existence. The gift is provided by a Creator who has willed to limit himself by giving us freedom, even the freedom to reject him. Such freedom is not something we can create or give or totally destroy. It is a gift of divine grace, offered freely by the One who is the Ground of our being.

It is a mistake, of course, to think that we have unlimited freedom. The range of choices available to us may be severely limited by many factors beyond our immediate control, such as illness, pain, economic need, or heredity. We may be limited by our own previous choices, which now determine the alternatives actually open before us. A bad habit freely chosen in the beginning may now control us. We are also limited in the time available for choices to be made. As Pascal once noted, our freedom is like the toss of a coin. We are free to call, but we must call before the coin hits the ground. All these limiting factors were present in one form or another in the death agonies of Ivan Ilyitch. But at the center of his existence he discovered an area of real freedom. He had the power of contrary choice on vital issues involving his immediate situation and his ultimate destiny. His use of this freedom made a crucial difference in the last hours of his life and in his death.

The potential grandeur of man is possible only because our freedom is real. We are free to make something of life. We are free to affirm the meaningfulness of existence even in an age of despair. We are free to grow in creative self-acceptance and self-fulfillment. We are free to relate to others in dynamic and mutually helpful ways. We are free to become whole persons, integrated persons, life-affirming persons. All this we are free to do because of God's gracious gift, actual freedom to choose from among the values given in our experience. But if this potential grandeur of man is authentic, how do we account for the incredible fact that we have all chosen misery rather than grandeur, enervating estrangement from God rather than fulfilling fellowship with him?

B. BASIC BELIEF

The only way to account for this fact is to come to grips with the problem of sin. Christians believe in the reality of sin because the freedom that makes it possible for us to choose God also makes it possible for us to reject him. We may choose to rebel against God, to ignore him, to live as if he didn't exist. Such choices, if followed to the bitter end, result in the destruction and annihilation of the self. But still the choice is ours, for God does not withdraw our freedom or force us to love him.

It is this voluntarily chosen rebellion against God we call sin. No single factor in human existence is more destructive, because sin leads to our estrangement from the Ground of our being. Estrangement from the Ground of our being means that life is distorted, frustrated, thwarted, and broken. It means that the self cannot achieve life-affirming wholeness because it is denying the very structure of reality. There is no problem in our human situation more serious than this problem of sin, the estrangement of ourselves from the Ground of our being.

When Christians speak of sin, they are not referring to mere isolated acts of disobedience or dishonesty, serious as these may be. Such isolated acts or desires are often called sins, but they are actually manifestations of sin, the state of conscious or subconscious rebellion against God.

Sin is the condition of the self when it has turned away from God, the source of its health and well-being. It is a disruption of the divinely intended bond between God and man. It is alienation from Ultimate Reality, separation from the Ground of our being. It is the willful elevation of ourselves to a position that belongs only to God. It is the refusal to acknowledge that we are finite and totally dependent upon God. It is the attempt to live with the gods of our own making rather than with the true and living God.

This has never been illustrated more effectively than in the familiar narrative about Adam and Eve (Gen., chs. 2 to 3). Most modern Christians have moved beyond the historical problems of these chapters to the truth about every man ("Adam" means "man") at the heart of the story. When God created man he intended him to live in a loving relationship with his Creator, a fact symbolized in the idea of a garden paradise. In order to remain "in paradise," man needed only to trust his Creator and obey him, as shown in the command not to eat the fruit of certain trees. But man refused to trust and obey. He wanted to be "like God," not in the creative role of one who reflects God's life, but in the destructive role of one who defies God and tries to become God. Man's disobedience, his rebellion against God, is symbolized in his eating of the fruit. As a result, man became estranged from God (expulsion from the Garden of Eden) and experienced depths of loneliness and suffering that he had never known before. This is truly the story of every man.

Contemporary theologians and psychologists, attempting to describe the conditions that lead to man's rebellion against God, have emphasized anxiety and temptation. Anxiety is the general state of depression and dis-ease caused by our finite condition. We are not in control of life and we know that death is inevitable; hence, we are the victims of gnawing distress about the future. Anxiety and fear often appear together, but they are not the same. When we are afraid, we can usually recognize the cause, but the causes of anxiety are deep and nameless. Paul Tillich's emphasis on anxiety about death, guilt, and meaninglessness has had a profound effect on recent theology, but it is extremely difficult to isolate such factors in our conscious life.

If anxiety is the inner precondition of sin, temptation usually presents the occasion. We are tempted whenever we are induced to seek escape from anxiety by obtaining security in something other than the true Ground of our security. Temptations abound in modern life, and even the most single-minded persons often underestimate the power of these temptations. We tend to have an exaggerated estimate of our own power to resist, an estimate that proves our undoing. One of my friends cleverly trained a pet dog named Clipper to demonstrate "the power of self-control." Clipper, who greatly relished cheese, was commanded to lie down. A savory piece of cheese was then placed on his extended paws with the words, "This is in trust." Clipper, seemingly aware of the power of temptation, almost broke his neck turning his head away. He wanted his nose as far from the source of temptation as possible. Only when given permission would he turn and finish the prize in one enormous canine gulp.

How often I have thought about this when contemplating our human tendency to nuzzle up to temptation, getting as close to it as possible, forgetting how our inner anxiety ill prepares us to resist.

But why can't anxiety and temptation lead us to throw ourselves in trust upon God rather than to reject him? If we are aware of our weakness and our need, why do we choose to rebel and make matters worse? Traditionally, Christian writers have singled out pride as the chief cause of our rebellion. When a Calvin or Niebuhr speak of pride, however, they do not mean mere conceit, though conceit is a common human failing. Frank Lloyd Wright once appeared in court as a witness and was asked, "Are you the greatest architect in the world?" He calmly replied, "Yes, I am." When his wife later reprimanded him, he protested, "But I was under oath—I had to tell the truth!" Such conceit may amuse us, but it is only one facet of the pride that causes our downfall.

Pride is essentially "playing God," trying to find ultimate security in the self alone, refusing to acknowledge our dependence upon our Creator. It is a condition of self-elevation that began when as children we found ourselves at the center of the world as we experienced it. Growth in maturity involves acceptance of the fact that we are not the center of the world. But we become deeply conditioned to this way of thinking and we are confirmed in it by anxious people around us who have not found their way into a God-centered existence. As a result, we are soon hopelessly embedded in this self-deceiving condition.

When we understand the nature of pride as self-elevation, we can also understand the inner meaning of the term "original sin." Pride is *the* original sin in each one of us, because it is logically and naturally first in the life of every man. Out of it stems both our growing rebellion against God and the specific acts of disobedience that are manifestations of our rebellion. Those who think of original sin as something that is "handed down" are partially correct, because we are deeply influenced by the vast complex of sin created by past generations and by contemporary society. This complex of sin tends to increase our anxiety and confirm our tendency to elevate ourselves to a position of independence that belongs only to God.

One of the most encouraging trends in current religious thought is the growing recognition of the seriousness of sin. Part of this has come from the incredible evidence of what man can do and be, apart from a creative relationship with God. While watching trainloads of Jewish children being torn from their parents and shipped away, François Mauriac turned to his wife and said, "We have just witnessed the end of an era." He meant the end of an era when we could believe in the fundamental goodness of man apart from God, the end of an era when we could rely upon man's ability to solve either personal or social problems on his own. Added to this is the minute by minute possibility of atomic disaster from which no man escapes, further evidence of the destructive potential of human life when men are estranged from God.

This new awareness of sin's destructive power partly accounts for the renewed interest in the apostle Paul. Few persons in history have struggled more vigorously with the problem of sin. Evidence of the struggle is in all his writings, but the most direct statement occurs in the seventh chapter of Romans, a deeply moving description of his inability to escape from the hold that sin had upon his life. Paul discovered that wanting to be good and knowing the good are never enough. His most poignant lament is that even when he knew what was good he could not do it! Hopelessly entangled in sin, inexorably moving toward a complete breakdown, Paul cried out in despair: "Wretched man that I am! Who will deliver me from this body of death?"

Many modern writers confidently answer, "No one!" It is at least to their credit that men such as Camus, Sartre, and O'Neill often exhibit a deeper awareness of the seriousness of man's predicament than many so-called believers. Jean-Paul Sartre, for instance, is extremely realistic in *No Exit,* a searing play about three people who have been condemned to hell. Hell in this case is a comfortable room with no exit. The three persons soon discover that each one will make a hell out of the situation for the others because each is incurably self-centered. "Hell is other people," Sartre concludes—other people who, like ourselves, are in proud rebellion against God. Estranged from God, they are inevitably estranged from one another. Sartre is correct in insisting that we cannot save ourselves, nor can other people save us. Who, then, can deliver us?

C. Beyond Belief: Fullness of Life

For Christian faith, the answer is clear. Before the echoes of his own question had died away, Paul exultantly shouted the answer, "Thanks be to God through Jesus Christ our Lord!" The same God who created man and gave him freedom, the same God who called man into creative communion with himself: this same God continues to act graciously toward us even in our rebellion. Through Jesus Christ he has offered to us in our estrangement the gift of reconciliation with himself. The incredible good news about this gift is at the center of the Christian's gospel and explains his burning desire to share the gift with the world. It is now possible for every man to achieve the purpose for his creation!

The New Testament makes it abundantly clear that the beginning of reconciliation comes when we recognize the seriousness of sin's hold upon us and feel sorrow for it. This involves much more than thinking about it. Even correct theological concepts are not enough. There must come a moment when we acknowledge our estrangement from God and long for a new life of communion with him. This is known as repentance, though in our state of self-elevation we despise the very word and its implied self-humiliation. Yet repentance is the first step on the way to reconciliation with God, the opening door into affirmative fullness of life.

The Greek word for repentance means literally "to change one's views" or "to change one's mind." This change usually begins with a frank recognition of sin for what it is. We stop trying to pretend that this is not a serious problem for us; we stop making excuses for ourselves; we stop attempting to cover up the destructive consequences of our sin. A classic Italian novel, *The Betrothed,* contains a vivid description of a plague that ravaged the city of Milan. At first the citizens, almost hysterical with fear, refused to face the fact that the plague was really among them. They punished anyone who spoke of it, insisting that it was only a pestilential fever. Later, they admitted it was a plague, but not the real plague. Finally, when people were dying by the score, they announced it was the real plague and took steps to bring it under control. In a similar way, the crucial turning point in human life comes when we openly acknowledge that we are infected with sin and take steps to bring it under control. This is part of what Camus was trying to tell modern society in his haunting novel *The Plague.*

Repentance also involves deep sorrow for the evil consequences of our past sin and a resolve to amend our ways. We are "heartily sorry for these our misdoings," so sorry that we take whatever steps are necessary to purify life and walk in holy obedience. This may involve breaking old habits, changing environment, establishing new patterns of daily conduct, and seeking reconciliation with those whom we have wronged. This change of life, this newness of direction, includes every area of life without exception. Martin Luther obviously realized the importance of total repentance, because the first principle of the famous Ninety-five Theses that he nailed to the door of the church reads as follows: "Our Lord and Master, Jesus Christ, in saying, 'Repent ye,' intended that the whole life of believers should be penitence."

A few acts of penitence are never enough, Luther is saying, when the whole life cries out for change.

Finally, repentance includes a longing for forgiveness. When we are acutely aware of how self-elevation has thwarted the creative self-fulfillment God intends for us, we are eager for a righting of the wrong. We "hunger and thirst" for the relationship with God that will give life meaning. But we know that our fellowship with God must be initiated and completed from God's side. We turn and place ourselves in a position to be forgiven, we long for it from the depths of our being, but it is God who must forgive. The incredible good news that he does forgive is really the heart of the Christian message and takes us beyond our present discussion of estrangement into a confrontation with the fact of divine grace.

We have seen already, however, the amazing possibilities of new life in Christ. It is creative and affirmative, openly rejoicing in freedom and in the healing that comes through repentance. It is a life that has come to a crucial turning place, a life pointed in a new direction, a life that has just caught sight of the dawn.

When Samuel Johnson was a young boy, he once refused to help his father because he was too proud to be seen doing menial work in his father's bookstall. But Johnson's memory of this disobedience haunted him all his life. When he was an old man, eager to make atonement, he made his way back to the market-place, standing for a while in the rain at the very spot where his father's stall had been. In describing the experience later, he said that he was never stronger than in that moment of honest repentance. But this is not surprising. We always receive new strength when we change the direction of our lives through repentance and find ourselves trembling on the threshold of reconciliation with God.

CHAPTER 3

Grace

An elderly minister once tried to tell me how he felt about the love of God by sharing a memorable experience. He and his wife had adopted a little girl from an unusually progressive orphanage many years before. Along with a carefully directed educational program, the institution held puppet shows, festivals, and other activities designed to keep the children happy. Mary, the little girl, adjusted quickly to her new home, but she insisted on visiting the orphanage as often as possible. On one of the visits in later years her father said to her, "I still don't understand why you were so glad to come and live with us when you enjoyed it so much here at the orphanage." "Oh," she replied quickly, "you don't understand. More than anything else I wanted someone to love me."

This is exactly how we feel when we come to the crucial turning point in our search for life's ultimate purpose. We need to know that we are accepted in spite of our rebellion and loved even when we have been unable to love. More than anything else we want someone to love us, but this is precisely the incredible good news of Christian faith. Even when we are most unlovable, there is yet One who loves us, and our ability to accept this love, to accept the fact that we are accepted by God, is the chief source of our physical, mental, and spiritual health and well-being.

41

A. Beyond Belief: God's Grace

The basic theme of the Biblical faith is not man's love for
God, but God's love for man. It is not primarily a record of
man's search for God, but God's search for man. The Creator
in the Old Testament is also the Redeemer who acts in history
to fulfill his loving purpose for man, and even Israel's flagrant
unfaithfulness cannot thwart his redemptive activity. The New
Testament writers continue this theme by insisting that God
has "come" into history in Jesus the Christ. Here is the supreme
revelation of God's intention for human life. When men tried to
block this divine act by killing the Christ, God used the death
to reveal his redemptive love for all men. Even at the end of the
Biblical record God is still "speaking" to the world through the
community of love that came into being as a result of the Christ
event. Here is the story of a God who acts! When Thomas
Carlyle asked a friend about the nature of God, the friend said
that he had to believe in a God who acts. Carlyle shouted: "Non-
sense! God does nothing!" Biblical writers, on the other hand,
are certain that God has done and is doing something of decisive
importance in human history.

Many modern Christians hesitate to speak of God's coming,
seeking, searching, or acting. This implies that he is "out there"
someplace and has to "come into the world," when actually he
is within the depths of our existence. To use Dietrich Bonhoeffer's
phrase, he is the Beyond who is within. We will have much more
to say about this problem of religious language. But the truth is,
Christians continue to speak of God's coming because this best
expresses one vital aspect of authentic religious experience.

Those who have moved into the new kind of life which
Christian faith makes possible describe it as a gift that has come
from God. It is something God has done, something God has
offered, something God has initiated. It comes to us, often when
we least expect it, sometimes when we are trying to escape. But

it is the very nature of God to "seek and to save that which is lost."

The parables of Jesus about the lost sheep and the lost coin both symbolize this truth about Ultimate Reality (Luke 15:3–10). Those who take the stories too literally and protest about the picture of a God who has to look for lost objects miss the point. God is obviously neither a shepherd nor a human being at all. But Christians are convinced that Ultimate Reality is concerned about individuals, seeks those who are in estrangement, and enters into the conscious lives of persons with the offer of forgiving love.

One news story that appeared in a popular magazine movingly reflects this same idea. A large family arrived one morning at a campsite near a stream in a national forest. After telling the older children to watch the younger ones, the parents concentrated on unpacking the car. At mealtime they called the children together and everyone came but Cathy. The blond, blue-eyed little three-year-old was missing. They called her name and searched for her to no avail. In desperation the father dived into the stream and searched along the bottom, fearing she might have tumbled in. As the hours passed, other campers came to join the anguished parents in looking for Cathy. Finally they found her, frightened but unharmed, in the bottom of a ravine. Everyone rejoiced that she was safe, but little Cathy best expressed the mood of the hour when they had all returned home that evening. Her father tucked her into bed and was leaving the room when Cathy suddenly said, "Gee, Daddy, aren't you glad you found me!"

Cathy, if you only knew! Think of a father's joy at finding his lost child! But Jesus said God is like that. God never stops seeking those who are lost in estrangement from him and he is glad when the lost are found.

There is something even more amazing about the essential nature of God as revealed in Jesus Christ. He not only comes to men in the midst of their estrangement and rebellion, but he comes as forgiving love. He offers men reconciliation with himself. He calls men into a creative relationship with himself in spite of their former rebellion. This is illustrated in an unsurpassed way in the story of the prodigal son, probably the best-known parable of Jesus' (Luke 15:11–32). When we leave home (rebellion) and try to live in the far country (estrangement), we end up in despair. But when we come to ourselves and turn toward home (repentance) we find a loving father waiting to forgive us. The father's forgiving love is the key to the story, the love that makes possible a new beginning and a new life for the son.

In the Bishop's Garden at the Washington Cathedral in the nation's capital, there is a contemporary sculpture of the prodigal and his father at the moment of reconciliation. The father's arms are extended over his son in forgiveness while the boy's arms reach up in repentance and acceptance. The two figures are cut out of the same block of stone so skillfully that they are blended into one another. It is impossible to tell where one ends and the other begins. This unity of form is a symbol of the reconciliation which has taken place between the two, a reconciliation made possible by the father's love.

Many Christians find their own deepest experience perfectly reflected in this simple story. The same God who is the Ground of our being is One who forgives his sons without exception. When we least deserve it, he "covers us" with his love, heals us, and offers us new life. How can we describe the essential nature of such a God? This is the serious problem we will face in the next section. The reality itself is beyond mere belief and beyond the grasp of limited human language. But those to whom the forgiving love of God has come know that it is authentic and that it is the most important single factor in the human quest for ultimate meaning.

B. BASIC BELIEF

The word "grace" is often used by Christians to describe the essential nature of God. The term generally refers to "a favor offered above that which is expected or deserved." In Christian thought it is a way of describing the forgiving love of God, which always comes to us as something more than we expect or deserve. His love for us is a "covering love," overflowing and spontaneous, unconditional and unmerited. It is an "abounding love" that takes us by surprise, a redeeming love that heals us and fills us with radiant joy.

It is often difficult to speak about such love in the modern world because the scientific revolution has destroyed the symbolic value of certain words and phrases of the past. A parallel revolution in religious language is taking place as Christians search for new ways of expressing their deepest convictions about God and the new life in Christ. We have already observed the widespread reticence about saying that God "comes to us," because this implies that he is off somewhere until he chooses to come. There is similar hesitation in speaking about our belief in "a" God, as if he were a Being over against the world, when in reality he is Being-itself. Such a phrase as "Being-itself" also helps us avoid saying that God is "up there" or "out there," ideas totally inacceptable to a generation acutely aware of outer space. "I didn't find God out there," said the Russian cosmonaut, and we are not amused, partly because his caustic comment confronts us with the inadequacy of current religious terminology.

But if he is not out there or up there, where is he? If he is not "a" God, a Being over against the world, who is he? How can we speak about God to a generation racing for the moon? How can our conversation about God be made relevant in a world that has come of age? When we examine the thought of Tillich, Bonhoeffer, and others who have written most helpfully on the

subject, we discover a turning within. Undoubtedly influenced by
the findings of dynamic psychology, they are looking within
the depths of man's inner experience for clues to the essential
nature of God. Hence, they refer to God as the Beyond that is
within, the Ground of our being, or as Being-itself. Instead of
being out there, he is at the center of life. He is not One who
comes from beyond, but Being-itself welling up within the un-
fathomable depths of our existence. As a mountain lake is fed
deep down by hidden springs that no man sees, so human life
is fed by the hidden springs of God's love from deep within.

There is no suggestion that we avoid "picture thinking" in
this new terminology. All human language involves reference
to time and space, and thus can never adequately describe the
God who is Ground of time and space. But the new depth "pictures" are more relevant and meaningful for modern man. For
example, the term "Father," which Jesus used most often in
referring to God, now becomes more intelligible. If we think of
God as "a" Father up there, it is difficult to avoid the Father-
on-a-cloud image of childhood. Instead, we may say that Being-
itself is like a father, ultimately loving, benevolent, concerned.
We may trust ourselves to Ultimate Reality, knowing that we
are loved, accepted, and forgiven. The Ground of all existence
is best described in terms of grace. When we really stop to think
about it, this is what Jesus was trying to tell us when he spoke
of God as "our Father."

This is also what Christian thinkers have been saying when
they refer to God as the Supreme Person. He is not a Person
over against other persons, but the Ground of all personal reality.
Since personal reality is the highest and most inclusive category
available to human thought, this is the highest and most inclusive
thing that can be said about God. When we say that God is
personal, we obviously do not fully encompass his essential nature, but this is the most that finite beings can say about him.

Ultimate Reality is at least personal reality, hence the possibility of grace at the center of existence.

But how do we know that God actually exists? Fortunately, the whole ground of this argument has shifted radically in recent years. Traditional theology spent a great deal of time trying to prove the existence of God with rational arguments. Ontological, cosmological, and teleological arguments were laboriously constructed, but as Kant demonstrated, they never really proved anything. On the contrary, the whole process implies that God might not exist. Why not begin by defining God as Ultimate Reality? Every thoughtful person knows that something is ultimate. The whole question then is not whether Ultimate Reality exists, but what Ultimate Reality is really like. The Christian is simply saying that he has experienced Ultimate Reality as unconditional, forgiving love, and that this fact is the most important single fact of his existence.

Why is it so important? What does the reality of grace at the center of existence actually mean to the individual? It means that his life-destroying estrangement from God can be overcome through an experience of reconciliation. This reconciliation with God made possible by divine grace is the basic experience of the Christian religion. "The origin and essence of all Christian life," says Bonhoeffer, "are comprised in the one process or event which the Reformation called justification of the sinner by grace alone." Through this process or event the individual moves into a life-affirming relationship with the Ground of his being. He comes to have a new appreciation for his own potential selfhood, and he begins to relate to the world of material things and to other persons in new and creative ways. His life is so rich and new that he looks back and hardly recognizes the person he was before. But this is not surprising, since he has literally become a new being through the power of God's healing grace at the center of his existence.

Because this basic experience is so rich, many terms have been used to describe it. Unfortunately, this multiplicity of terms tends to destroy the essential simplicity of Christian belief at this point. Some persons erroneously think of the Christian life as a kind of fraternal order in which the candidate advances through many stages toward perfection. The stages are reconciliation, justification, new birth, regeneration, salvation, conversion, and redemption. But these are not different experiences or even different stages of one experience. They are simply varying ways of describing one fundamental experience of Christian faith, the establishment of the God-man relationship through which the ultimate purpose for human life is realized. This simple relationship, made possible through the grace of God, is the pearl of great price, the treasure hidden in a field, the one thing needful in every human life.

Reconciliation, a term often used in the New Testament and in contemporary medical psychology, is especially effective in conveying the idea of a restored relationship. *Justification* is a word that appears often in the writings of Paul and the Protestant Reformers. It is taken from the law courts, where a man stands guilty before the judge, awaiting sentence. Through the "grace" of the judge, the offender is "reckoned" as righteous or justified, not through anything he has done to deserve it, but through grace alone. *New birth* is discussed by Jesus and Nicodemus in the Gospel of John and refers to the need for men to be born again. Every individual is born once into a physical existence, but he must also be born into the life of the Spirit, where he is at one with God's purpose for his life. It is interesting to note that the Greek phrase used in John actually means "born from above," thus emphasizing that this new life is from God. *Regeneration* is essentially another way of describing new birth.

Salvation is a more general term for this fundamental Christian experience, referring especially to the way the individual is "saved" from estrangement and delivered into a new life with

God. *Conversion* emphasizes the "turning around" or "turning about" of the individual from his old life of rebellion to his new life in Christ. *Redemption,* another idea used by Paul, is taken from the ancient slave market, where a slave on the block discovers to his amazement that someone has paid the purchase price and set him free. In this same way an individual who is enslaved by sin is set free through the grace of God.

In the next section of this chapter we will discuss the response of faith required of the individual in this basic Christian experience, but we cannot emphasize too strongly the priority of grace. Christians in every age have insisted that their new life in Christ is not something they achieved, but something they have received from God as a gift of grace. In the phrase used by C. S. Lewis to describe his own Christian experience, we are "surprised by joy."

I can remember trying to explain this to a group of college students in the coffeehouse on a night when the newspapers were filled with the story of an overseas airliner that had gone down in mid-Atlantic. In a sudden nightmare of terror, the passengers found themselves in pitch-darkness, tossed about on tiny rafts by hundred-foot waves. One survivor, a retired Army captain, later told of watching his own wife disappear, unable to help her in the confusion. "I never saw her again," he said. "I thought I was going to die. I was certain we were all going to die. Our situation was utterly hopeless. Then suddenly we saw the lights of a ship, and those lights were the most welcome sight I have ever seen!" He finally broke off in silence after trying to tell reporters what the lights of a rescue ship meant to those who were lost in total darkness in the mid-Atlantic, utterly without hope in the world. Their joy and relief were beyond the power of words to describe.

I tried to tell the students that we feel this way when we perceive the saving light of God's grace "coming" into the darkness of our estrangement and despair. Tossed about by forces beyond our control, unable to see any signs of hope, filled with anxiety and fear, we are suddenly saved. We are saved by something that comes to us, something given to us, something that is beyond us. The Beyond may confront us within the deep center of our own lives, as many theologians are insisting, but it is a Beyond we experience as a saving power greater than ourselves. It is not surprising that Christians still sing with exultant joy about the "amazing grace" of God.

C. BEYOND BELIEF: FULLNESS OF LIFE

In this mood the author of Ephesians cried out to his fellow Christians, "By grace you have been saved through faith; and this is not your own doing, it is the gift of God" (Eph. 2:8). The statement that we are saved by grace *through* faith points in the direction of man's responsibility in this event. The individual enters into the fullness of life that reconciliation makes possible when he responds to God's grace in faith.

Few persons fully appreciate the uniqueness of the Christian life in this respect. Adherents of other religions are given a set of rules or laws to guide them in their religious life. By obedience to the rules the individual earns the favor of God and is "accepted" or rewarded by him. Those who disobey are punished or rejected by God. This view is often called legalism because it emphasizes salvation through strict conformity to law.

I can vividly remember visiting an impressive Islamic mosque in the Egyptian city of Cairo. Our host was a zealous young disciple of Muhammad. With radiant face he explained the five religious duties imposed on every good Muslim. By faithfully practicing these duties, he assured us, the Muslim remains in the favor of Allah. Similarly, the disciples of other religions are instructed in what they must do in order to find favor with God.

Unfortunately, there is a widespread tendency for Christianity to lapse into this kind of legalism. Many Roman Catholics, performing religious chores, and many Protestants, active in the program of the church, feel that they are winning favor with God by living a "good" life. This feeling has been strengthened by the teaching that we go to heaven as a reward when our good works outweigh the bad.

In view of this tragic misunderstanding, it is highly encouraging to find twentieth-century Protestantism rediscovering the basic truth of reconciliation "by grace through faith." For what the Christian discovers to his great joy is that he does not have to earn the favor of God. In fact, he soon realizes that no person can ever make himself good enough to deserve God's love. The incredible good news is that God already loves every person without exception. This means that we are reconciled to him, not through making ourselves worthy of his love, but simply by a faith response to that love, by "having faith" in that love.

What having faith means is clearly illustrated in the first sermon of Jesus as reported by Mark (ch. 1:14–15). According to this record, Jesus "came into Galilee, preaching the gospel of God." After announcing that the Kingdom of God is at hand, Jesus gave his hearers specific instructions about how to accept it. "Repent," he said, "and believe in the gospel."

In the last chapter we discussed the necessity of repentance as the first step into the new life with God. But repentance alone is never enough. It must be followed by the full acceptance of God's forgiving love. Jesus said, "Believe in the gospel." The word "gospel" in this case means good news about God's love. The word "believe" includes intellectual belief in God's love, but means much more than this. It involves the trustful acceptance of God's love by the whole person, by the total being, "with all your heart, and with all your soul, and with all your strength, and with all your mind." When we respond in faith, we stop trying to save ourselves and make ourselves good enough to be saved by God. We simply repent of our rebellion against him and fully accept the healing power of his grace. We yield

ourselves unconditionally to the divine love offered to us unconditionally. We hear the divine word of invitation and we obey
without reservation. When we believe (trust, accept) the good
news of God's love in this way, we find that God, through his
grace, makes all things new within us and in our relationship
to all created things and persons.

In Christian thought, many questions have arisen about this
fundamental act of faith. Is it, for example, something we do
once in a decisive way or is it a continuing experience? It is
both. This is why Bonhoeffer spoke of it as an event and as a
process. In one respect it is a once-and-for-all event, transforming
life so completely that we are never the same again. It is a
decision in which we recognize the significance of our faith
relationship with the Ground of our being and consciously
decide for it. But it is also a continuing process, one that goes
on throughout life. Every day of my life, anxiety leads me to
rebel against God. Every day, therefore, I need to repent and
accept the love of God, thus "growing in grace" moment by
moment.

Can I expect my faith response to result in a sudden and
dramatic conversion, or will it come gradually and quietly? It
may come either way. For the apostle Paul, it was a violent
traumatic experience, because he had been trying so hard to save
himself through obedience to the law. Nothing less than a
violent turning would do. Similarly, persons who have been in
wild rebellion against God need "breaking" before they are ready
for healing. Others, on the other hand, may have grown up in
Christian homes where they come very gradually to the full
acceptance of reconciliation with God. Even in these individuals,
however, there must be a moment of definite decision, a time
when this thing which has been happening over a long period
is consciously and fully accepted. Sometimes we are told that
the faith of children is unfolding like a flower, but, alas, the
plant withers and the bloom never appears!

Another continuing question in Christian thought arises out of the unique relation of faith and works in redemption. Because Paul preached salvation by faith so persuasively, there were some in the early church who believed good works had no place in the Christian life. The Letter of James was written to protest this misunderstanding of the Christian position. Good works, the author insists, are the inevitable outgrowth of salvation by faith, so essential that we may question the validity of any Christian life in which they do not appear. By their fruits you shall know them. The important point, however, is that good works are not performed in order to be saved, but *because* we have been saved. We love because we have been loved by God.

An exciting development in contemporary religion is the creative insight that medical psychology contributes to all these aspects of the Christian experience of reconciliation. Psychology has shown, for example, that the neurotic person cannot save himself. The more he struggles alone, the more he becomes entwined in his own problem. The more he tries to follow the advice of well-meaning friends and "get hold of himself," the more frustrated and defeated he feels. The individual must be willing to seek help outside of himself. This help often begins with his physician, minister, or friend. But the deepest healing comes when he accepts "help" from God and relates himself to the meaningful structure of reality. Accepting help from God, trusting himself to the meaningful structure of reality, is simply another way of describing the Christian's acceptance of grace by faith.

Medical psychology has also shown the necessity of creative self-affirmation on the part of the individual. We cannot function properly when we hate ourselves. Unfortunately, some Christian preaching has condemned rebellious self-elevation in ways that lead persons to feel they must hate and reject themselves in order to be saved. On the contrary, when we begin to experience the power of God's forgiving love, we cannot help having a new estimate of ourselves. Awareness of God's love leads to a whole new positive feeling about our potential selfhood. Our shame over what we have been is overshadowed by the jubilation over what we may become. Thus we are able to affirm our own worth under God. This creative self-affirmation, one of the most important factors in psychological health, is an integral part of the Christian experience of reconciliation.

Throughout this section on the fullness of the new life in Christ we have been emphasizing the place of human responsibility. The response of faith is essential. But here, as elsewhere, grace has the last word, for the Christian knows that even his faith is a gift of God's grace. It is God who gives us the desire and the power to respond in faith. Our freedom is real, the choice is always ours, but the power to make the creative choice is a gift from God. "By grace you have been saved through faith; and this is not your own doing, it is the gift of God."

The Christian can never stop rejoicing in the wonder of the grace that has saved him. He can never stop telling others about it because he wants to share it with everyone he meets. This grace is the heart of the Christian's good news, the source of meaningfulness in every area of his life, and the ground of his hope for the future. It is no wonder Christians are such joyful people, for they have been grasped by grace and reconciled with the Ground of all being.

The earliest prayers that my own children learned were prayers of gratitude. Little Kathleen was unusually adept at "thank you God" prayers, especially when she found that long prayers delayed the hour of sleep. She often prayed for every child she knew: "Thank you, God, for Mary and Susie and John and Billy," and on and on. Then she would take a deep breath and begin again, "Thank you, God, for Mary's Mommy and Daddy, and Susie's Mommy and Daddy," until everyone's Mommy and Daddy had been included. I am sure her Heavenly Father never lost patience, but her earthly father certainly did!

Some nights, however, when Kathleen was very tired and anxious to sleep, her prayers would move to the other extreme. She would close her eyes and say simply, "Thank you, God, for God. Amen."

When a Christian who has been confronted by Ultimate Reality as saving grace enters into the fullness of life which that grace provides, his exultant prayer is the same. Thank you, God, for God. Amen.

CHAPTER 4

Incarnation

MODERN MAN is desperately waiting for Godot, but Godot never comes. This is the provocative theme of a drama by Samuel Beckett, a playwright who is exceedingly pessimistic about human existence. He is convinced that there is no hope for man unless someone comes to reveal the meaning of life, but he is equally certain no one will come. The action of *Waiting for Godot* is deceptively simple. Two tramps are on stage throughout the play, waiting for someone named Godot, obviously the author's symbol for God. They talk endlessly about how essential it is for him to come, but when the play ends, Godot has not come and we know that he will not come. Man waits in vain.

In one respect, Beckett is reflecting the mood of the New Testament, for the early Christians were just as certain about the need for some saving word from "beyond." The ultimate meaning of human existence must be revealed by someone who comes. In his pessimism about the coming of Godot, however, Beckett is marching directly against the full force of the New Testament witness. Every New Testament writer, every early Christian, was positively convinced that Godot had come! The long centuries of waiting were over. The messenger had arrived. The saving word had been spoken by One who came into human life for this very purpose. But the One who came was himself the message. This is both the meaning and the mystery of the incarnation.

A. Beyond Belief: God's Grace

Jesus Christ as the incarnation of God's grace stands at the heart of Christian faith. "Incarnation" is from a Latin word meaning "enfleshment" or "taking bodily form." To the Christian, it means that the innermost nature of Ultimate Reality has taken flesh and dwelt among us in human form. The divine grace that we have been emphasizing as the key to man's relationship with God is not simply an abstract concept or idea. This grace has appeared in human history, in our midst, in One who was truly one of us.

We must speak in the next section about how difficult it is to express this truth in conceptual terms. The difficulty, however, should not distract us from the central fact: in the beginning, Jesus Christ was not a doctrinal object of belief, but a Person whose presence was experienced. Someone had appeared among the early Christians to save them from their estrangement and reconcile them to God. As they struggled to find words to describe their experience, they often found themselves at odds with one another. But they were one in their conviction that the Christ event was the most important thing that had ever *happened to them.* That it had happened to them they never doubted for a moment.

The first time I visited the Italian city of Florence, I was especially impressed by the unfinished sculpture of Michelangelo on display in the Academy. In one huge block of marble, powerful half formed figures appear to be struggling to free themselves from the stone. The work, called *The Prisoners,* was intended to show the dignity of human beings, even when suffering in captivity. In their present unfinished form, the prisoners seem to be waiting for someone to come and liberate them, not only from their captivity, but from the very marble that imprisons them.

Before the coming of Christ, men were held captive by ignorance about life's purpose. They struggled to make life meaningful, but the divine intention had been only partially revealed. The human form was imprisoned by ignorance and by estrangement from the Ground of being. Human life, only half formed and partially realized, awaited the coming of the Master Sculptor who could complete it. The potential in human life awaited actualization. Captive men awaited freedom.

Then Jesus Christ came as the One who set men free by fulfilling the purpose for human existence in his own life and by making this fulfillment possible for others. In his presence, men "came to themselves" and began to achieve the fullness of their human destiny. Through him, humanity came into its own. In *Dr. Zhivago,* Boris Pasternak has written with deep feeling about the impact of Christ's coming upon our human situation. After describing the corruption of the Roman Empire, he says, "And then, into this tasteless heap of gold and marble, He came, light and clothed in an aura . . . and at that moment gods and nations ceased to be and man came into being—man the carpenter, man the plowman, man the shepherd with his flock of sheep at sunset, man who does not sound in the least proud, man thankfully celebrated in all the cradle songs of mothers and in all the picture galleries the world over. . . . Something in the world had changed. . . . Individual human life became the life story of God, and its contents filled the vast expanses of the universe."

From earliest times, Christians have felt this way about his coming. Something in the world has changed. New life is possible for every man, new life that brings us to our full stature as the children of God. For all who have experienced this new life, Christ's coming is the most important event in history. In the state of Oklahoma I met an American Indian pastor whose life was a radiant witness to this fact. His theology was very simple, the certainty of his faith unassailable. He described how some of his people were still bitter because of the way the white man had taken their land. But he said he was not bitter. "You took our land from us," he declared thoughtfully. "But you brought us Jesus Christ, and what would life be without Christ?"

All who have experienced God's grace in Christ share this conviction. Because of Christ's coming, the Father's love for us has become so real that nothing else matters in comparison with it. Yet at the same time everything matters more, matters in a new way, because all of life is seen in a new light. It is Jesus Christ who makes everything we have been saying about the divine intention for life possible. Life rich with meaning is not just a possibility. It is an actuality. Relationship with the Ground of our being is not just a concept. It is a reality. All this is true because Jesus Christ has come as the incarnation of the grace of God.

B. BASIC BELIEF

A study of theological history reveals the complexity of the church's continuing attempt to describe the precise meaning of Christ's coming. All Christian theology centers in the Christ, a fact symbolized by the place this chapter on Christ holds at the center of this book. But it is one thing to symbolize the centrality of incarnation and another to describe Christian belief about it in a relevant way.

Part of the problem arises because the incarnation appears to be a complete paradox. On the one hand, we are certain that Jesus Christ was truly human. The disciples experienced his presence as a human presence. He was one of them, born of a natural mother, growing in the normal way in a normal home. He hungered and grew thirsty. He laughed and wept. He became weary and slept. He had a man's consciousness, thinking and feeling about himself as a man does. He felt pain and suffered and died. He was in the fullest sense a human being. This is why Martin Luther could state confidently, "The beginning of all our theology is in the humanity of Jesus."

On the other hand, we are certain that Jesus Christ was truly divine. This same Luther declared, "To this One [Christ] thou shalt point and say, 'Here is God.'" Those who were in the presence of Christ knew that they were in the presence of God. They tried to explain this by saying that he was conceived by the Holy Spirit and even at an early age felt a call to be about his Father's business. They reported that he had healed the sick and raised the dead "by the finger of God." They remembered how his words had been filled with the divine life. "Never has any man spoken as he speaks!" Though he suffered, he was transfigured before them. Though he was killed, he rose again from the dead. This is the paradox. The One who was a human being was at the same time truly divine.

How can we explain such a paradox? How can one person be human and divine? For centuries the church has struggled with this problem, formulating a head-swimming array of creeds and theological definitions. Most of these have proved unsatisfactory because they were attempts to force two natures or two substances or two persons into one. Inevitably, they leaned too far in one direction or another, thus compromising either the humanity or the divinity of Christ.

When Apollinaris, for example, said that the divine reason took the place of a finite rational soul in Jesus, he was denying any real humanity. The Adoptionists, on the other hand, said that Jesus was a true human being who had been adopted and perfected by God. This was rejected as a denial of any divinity "in the beginning," a truth about which the Gospel of John is quite explicit. The most famous controversy centered around a brilliant fourth-century scholar named Arius whose position has been called "the greatest of the heresies." He taught that Jesus was neither God nor man, but an intermediate being, superior to man but subordinate to God. Under the leadership of the equally gifted Athanasius, Christian orthodoxy condemned such a view because it amounted to a denial of both the humanity and divinity of Christ.

As a result of these theological battles, the church was able to state its "official" position by A.D. 451 in the Creed of Chalcedon. The statement is no solution to the problem, however, for the Creed says simply that Christ is truly human, Christ is truly divine, Christ is one. How can this be? Even in modern times, unsuccessful attempts are often made to answer this question by forcing the two natures of Christ into one person. A whole new approach to the problem is now possible, however, thanks to the combined efforts of medical psychology and contemporary theology. The new approach may be called the dynamic-relational view because the emphasis is upon the dynamic relation that existed between Christ and God.

We have been emphasizing throughout our discussion the key to the meaning of human existence found in man's relationship to God. When a man is most fully and meaningfully related to God, the Ground of his being, he is most fully and meaningfully himself. He is a true human being, a whole person, one who is realizing the divine intention for his life. This relationship, as we have seen, is not something that man establishes from his side. It is a relationship initiated and established by a free gift of God's grace. Man must accept, however, because grace does not force, grace does not compel. An act of faith is required of man. The full meaning of human life is realized therefore in the meeting (relationship) between God's grace and man's faith.

Jesus Christ is the incarnation, the manifestation in human form, of this grace-faith relationship which is the key to all human existence. He is the supreme example of the God-man relationship for which every person has been created. He is

truly divine because he represents the most complete movement
of God's grace into human life, a movement of the God who
called Christ into relationship with himself and revealed the
ultimate purpose for life. Christ is truly human because his life
is the fullest response that man can make to God, a free, total,
loving response to the action of God's grace in his life.

We have said first that his life represents the most complete
movement of God's grace into human life. The eternal dimension
of this movement is symbolized in the idea of the preexistent
Christ as set forth in the first chapters of John and Colossians.
This does not refer to the preexistence of the earthly life of
Jesus, but to the expression of God's grace toward men "in the
beginning" and ever since. The incarnation in Jesus Christ of
this self-expressive grace of God is symbolized throughout the
New Testament in many ways. He was conceived by the Holy
Spirit. He heard God's voice at his baptism saying, "This is my
beloved Son." He was able to mediate God's grace directly to
others in his ministry of teaching and healing. Signs and wonders
were experienced by many who were in his presence. At the
Mount of Transfiguration, in Gethsemane, and on the cross,
God's grace empowered him and spoke through him to others.
Finally, God raised him from the dead as the ultimate authenti-
cation of his entire life, a life that represents in every respect
the farthest reach of God's grace into our human situation.

We have also said that Jesus Christ represents the fullest response that human life can make to God. This is symbolized in
the beginning when Joseph and Mary bring their infant son to
the Temple for his "presentation" to God. This voluntary presentation of Jesus to God is one of the dominant themes of the
New Testament. At every point, Jesus responded to God's intention for his life with total obedience. He heard and obeyed
the word of God as it came to him during his baptism. He went
into the wilderness for a continuing encounter with God through
which he could clarify the divine calling that he had experienced.

He rejected all temptation to disobey the will of God. He spent long nights of vigil in prayer, seeking to understand the nature of God's claim upon his life and offering himself unconditionally. "He increased in wisdom and in stature, and in favor with God." "He learned obedience," surrendering himself creatively and affirmatively. He "emptied himself" and opened his life to the power of God until he could say, "I and the Father are one." Finally, in Gethsemane and on the cross his response was total and his affirmative surrender to God was absolute. "Not my will, but thine, be done." "Into thy hands I commit my spirit!"

We have now said that Jesus Christ is truly divine because he represents the most complete movement of God's grace into human life. We have also said that he is truly human because he represents the fullest response that human life can make to God. Those who read the New Testament with this double emphasis in mind will find it repeated innumerable times. John's Gospel, for example, opens with an overpowering Prologue describing the Word (self-expressive grace) of God which was "in the beginning" and became flesh to dwell among us. This same Gospel emphasizes at least fifty times that Christ lived in subordination to God. "I can do nothing on my own authority." "He who sent me is with me. . . . I always do what is pleasing to him." "This charge I have received from my Father." "For I have come down from heaven, not to do my own will, but the will of him who sent me." "Not I, but the Father."

The same double emphasis appears throughout the Pauline literature. In the first chapter of Colossians the idea of the preexistent Christ appears: "In him all things were created, in heaven and on earth, visible and invisible, whether thrones or dominions or principalities or authorities—all things were created through him and for him. He is before all things." The second chapter of Philippians, on the other hand, contains an overwhelmingly moving description of Christ's total obedience. "He emptied himself, taking the form of a servant, being born in the likeness of men. And being found in human form he humbled himself and became obedient unto death, even death on a cross."

The author of Hebrews is equally certain that God has truly spoken to men in Jesus the Christ. Jesus reflected the true glory of God and bore the very stamp of His nature. He was called and appointed by God to be the great High Priest to all men. Yet at the same time, Jesus was made like his brethren in every respect. He overcame temptation as other men overcome temptation and he learned obedience as other men learn obedience. "In the days of his flesh, Jesus offered up prayers and supplications, with loud cries and tears, to him who was able to save him from death, and he was heard for his godly fear. Although he was a Son, he learned obedience through what he suffered." (Heb. 5:7–8.) In similar fashion the other New Testament writers develop this double theme, the unconditional "coming" of God's grace in Christ and the unconditional response of Christ in obedience and trust.

Here is the traditional double insistence of Christianity upon the divinity and humanity of Christ, but not in a static form that tries to force two natures or two persons into one. Instead, the emphasis is on the dynamic relation between God and Jesus, between divine grace and human freedom. Here is the most complete action of God's grace in human life and the fullest free response that man can make to God. Here is the perfect "union" between God and man, the supreme example of the God-man relationship intended as the key to the meaning of human existence. Christ is the fulfillment of God's purpose for man and the fulfillment of man's capacity for God.

God calls all men and offers them his grace, but not in the same way or degree. He offers all men the grace to become his sons, for example, but only Christ was offered the grace to become *the* Son of God. Similarly, all men are called to total obedience, but no one approaches the degree of obedience offered to God by

Christ. Thus we may speak of Christ's utter uniqueness in both respects, in the offer of grace and in the free response, but he was not a different kind of being. He would not be our Savior unless he was truly one of us, but this is precisely what a Christology based on the dynamic relation between God and Jesus is saying. In Christ it is nothing other than God himself whom we meet, yet we meet him in a true man.

In him we see the actuality of that which, to a lesser degree, is the possibility for every human life. In him, God has actualized the creative God-man relationship intended for every person. The secret of our growth into true manhood is openly revealed in him. In this sense, *only Jesus Christ is truly human*. The rest of us are partially human, that is, partially fulfilling the true purpose and possibility of our humanity. The more fully we approximate the God-man relationship seen in Christ, the more truly human we become.

At this point, however, many persons are confronted by a stumbling block of serious proportions, because the New Testament writers insist that it was the death of Jesus that brought them most fully into this relationship with God. John says that God so loved the world that he *gave* his Son. Paul says that "God shows his love for us in that while we were yet sinners Christ died for us. . . . We were reconciled to God by the death of his Son. . . . At the right time Christ died for the ungodly." The author of Hebrews builds his whole book around Christ as the supreme High Priest who offered the supreme sacrifice, his own life, to make atonement for the sins of the world. But what does this mean, to say that Christ died for us? How can we be involved in a death that took place two thousand years ago?

The answer to these questions is contained in the Christian doctrine of the atonement. Atonement simply means at-one-ment with God. The doctrine of the atonement is an explanation of how Christ's death has brought about reconciliation (at-one-ment) between man and God. In general, three main theories of the atonement have developed in Christian history. Two of the three (ransom theory and substitutionary theory) are objective in nature, emphasizing what God has done in the crucifixion. The third (moral theory) is subjective in nature, emphasizing what we are moved to do by the crucifixion.

The ransom theory is the oldest. In one form or another it declares that through the death of Christ the hold of sin upon my life has been broken. God has overcome the power of evil. The substitutionary theory was first clearly formulated in the tenth century by Anselm, who insisted that sin is a dishonoring of God. Therefore, some satisfaction must be made to God, but the gravity of the sin and the infinite quality of God's honor make it impossible for me or any sinful human being to make worthy restitution to God. The only worthy sacrifice is Jesus Christ, God's own Son, who dies as a substitute for me.

There are two main strengths to these objective views. First, they clearly show that the atonement is an act of God, something that God has done to make reconciliation possible. Secondly, they recognize the costly nature of the atoning process, especially in the substitutionary theory, in which the cost of God's forgiveness is always stressed. It is reported that when the German poet Heine was dying, a friend tried to comfort him by telling him that God would forgive him. Heine snorted: "Forgive me? Of course he will forgive me. It's his business to forgive!" The substitutionary theory makes it clear that forgiveness is never this easy. There is a costliness about it which God reveals to men through the sacrificial death of his own Son.

The critical weakness in these objective theories is their failure to stress the relevance of the crucifixion for individuals in every generation. They turn the death of Jesus into a faraway cosmic event, something that God and Christ did entirely apart from us. The atonement becomes an act done for me, not an act requiring something of me. For this reason, the moral theory of the atonement was formulated by Abelard in the tenth century. Abelard insists that the important thing is the way the death of Jesus moves us to repent of our sins and accept the forgiving love of God. After discussing the nature of Christ's death, Abelard points out how "our hearts should be enkindled by such a gift of divine grace." The important thing is the enkindling of our hearts, the response of repentant trust that the death of Jesus evokes in us.

Christian thought through the ages has swung back and forth between the objective and subjective theories of atonement, but an adequate explanation of the cross event demands a recognition of the truth in both. The cross is, first of all, a cosmic event, a decisive act of God, something that God does to make reconciliation possible. The purpose of the act, however, is not fulfilled in my life until I respond through repentance and the acceptance of God's love for me.

The word "involvement" might be used to describe both the objective and subjective aspects of atonement. The cross is an act of God through which he reveals the extent of his involvement in the human situation. God does not accept man's rebellion as the last word. He does not leave man to suffer in his estrangement alone. God cares, God comes, God manifests his love for man through the total involvement of himself in man's life, even to the death of the One who fully revealed the divine intention for human life. In the cross of Christ the participation of God in our estrangement thus becomes fully manifest and the atoning love of God becomes fully known. At the same time, however, the cross calls forth my own total involvement in the atoning act of God. This total involvement moves me to repent of my rebellion and of my participation in the totality of human rebellion. It also moves me to accept fully the love of God that is so clearly revealed in this event. Atonement is thus a process of double involvement: the revealing of God's atoning purpose through his involvement in our human estrangement, and the response to God's atoning purpose called forth by our involvement in his atoning act.

The death of Christ is the climax of the incarnation event because it is the point of sharpest focus, the point at which God's purpose for man's life is most clearly seen. Many modern Christians have unfortunately missed this point of focus, due to the church's neglect of the doctrine of atonement. This is because many of the thought forms in which the doctrine was presented in the past are no longer meaningful. But the cross remains central, the climax of God's revealing grace in the incarnation, and it will not surprise us to find renewed interest in the atonement accompanying the renewal of the church in twentieth-century Christianity.

There is a very old church in Sweden with a striking crucifix on the wall opposite the pulpit. When visitors inquire why it wasn't placed in the front where the congregation could see it, they are told a strange story. Many years before, when the king of Sweden visited the church unexpectedly on a Sunday morning, the pastor departed from his prepared sermon and eulogized the honored visitor. A short time later the crucifix arrived as a gift from the king, with specific instructions to place it opposite the pulpit where the preacher would see it and remember what he was supposed to be talking about.

The cross is what Christians are supposed to be talking about, because it is the clearest disclosure of God's gracious purpose for human life, the supreme point of meeting in the relationship between God and man made possible through the incarnation.

C. Beyond Belief: Fullness of Life

The new life that the incarnation event makes possible for the individual may best be described as a life of discipleship. God sends Jesus Christ as the manifestation of his purpose for human life, and Jesus Christ calls men to discipleship. He does this in order to lead them into the fullness of life now possible for them because of his life (and death) among them. The call of Christ is not primarily a call to believe certain things, for even "the wise and understanding" may miss the hidden inner meaning of his coming. His call is to both wise and simple. It is a call to discipleship, a call for us to follow him. Through following him we enter into fullness of life, eternal life, life under the reign of God. This following him in discipleship involves both hearing and obedience.

Hearing means not only listening, but putting ourselves in a position to hear his call and his instruction. It means seeking to know about him, learning about his life and death, reading books about him (especially the New Testament), and meditating upon the meaning of his coming. Following Jesus includes "knowing about" the One whom we are following. Hearing his call and instruction also involves use of the traditional "means of grace" such as worship, sacraments, and participation in the Christian community. We do not use the means of grace in order to become good enough for God to love us, but because God does love us and calls us to obedience. We are eager to hear what this obedience means, because it is the only alternative to futility in our human existence, the only way to fullness of life. In the time of John Wesley a group of Moravians taught that a man who wanted reconciliation should do absolutely nothing to seek it. Since it was a gift of pure grace, they insisted, he should stop attending church, praying, reading the Bible, or taking the sacraments, and simply wait for God to act. Wesley categorically opposed this dangerous quietism, insisting that discipleship includes using every possible means of hearing God's word for our lives.

Hearing is thus the beginning of discipleship. It is then followed by the total obedience of the whole self to the call and instruction of God which we have heard in Christ. We seek obedience of body, mind, will, and emotion. Such obedience involves detachment of the self from everything but God. We are detached from money and material things, because no man can serve God and mammon. We are detached from pleasure as an end-in-itself, because a disciple must be willing to drink the cup of suffering. We are detached from self-elevation as an end-in-itself, because he who seeks to save his own life will lose it. We are detached from our loved ones, because he who loves mother and father, sister and brother, more than Christ cannot be his disciple. Detachment means dependence upon God alone. It means that we are ultimately concerned about God, the living God, the God who is the Ground of our being. We acknowledge that our relationship with this Ground of being is the one thing truly needful for life, the one thing for which we will sell and give up everything we have. Dietrich Bonhoeffer said that when Christ calls a man, he bids him come and die. This is correct. He bids him die to everything but God.

Detachment is one way of expressing the disciple's total obedience to God in Christ. Another way is best described as commitment or surrender to God and the things of God. It is singleness of purpose, seeking God first. The nature of such commitment is found in the teaching of Jesus and in the example of his own life. The Sermon on the Mount, contrary to much popular opinion, is not a "heavy burden" of law that Christ laid upon his followers. It is simply an illustration of the life of those who want to seek God above all things and ground their lives in the meaningful structure of reality. Christ himself is the supreme example of the life of obedience to God described in the Sermon.

The actual power to hear and obey the call to discipleship comes to the individual primarily through his participation in the Christian community, the church. We have said little about this community because we have been centering our attention upon the relationship between God and the individual, which is at the heart of Christian experience. But the individual cannot find the way alone. In actual practice we come into this relationship through involvement in the community of faith, the community of those who are growing in grace together. From this point, therefore, we begin emphasizing the role of the Christian community in the meaningful existence made possible by the Christ event.

Participation in the community is not only a practical necessity. It is also an inevitable outgrowth of the joy that Christians experience through obedience to Christ. Contrary to popular opinion, Christian discipleship does not involve a grim hatred of the self, the rejection of the self, or the destructive commitment of the self to another because of a desire for self-punishment. On the contrary, it is the obedience of the self, based upon an affirmative belief that God through Christ can make something of us. It is the obedience of a person affirmatively seeking the ultimate purpose for his existence. It is the creative surrender of the self to the meaningful structure of Ultimate Reality. It is the kind of obedience that leads to psychological health and well-being, for it is based upon affirmative belief in the value of the self as a child of God. Hence the joy of the Christian life, a joy inevitably shared with others in the community of God's people.

We have spent a great deal of time discussing the incarnation, because in it we find the clearest disclosure of God's ultimate purpose for human life. Christ's coming is the center of history for the individual and the world, the hinge upon which all meaningful existence turns. But the majority of men have not yet discovered this truth. As we suggested at the beginning of this chapter, the real irony of our human situation is that modern man knows he needs a saving word from beyond himself, but he does not know that the word has come.

Franz Kafka, a powerful literary figure of this century, wrote a parable called "An Imperial Message" that illustrates this perfectly. Imagine, he suggests, that the dying emperor has sent a message of life-and-death importance to you alone. The messenger sets out on his journey to bring you the message. He is a powerful and indefatigable man but he encounters overwhelming resistance at every step along the way. The multitudes are so vast he cannot make his way through them; the obstacles are so great he cannot surmount them. Vainly he wears out his strength, only to find himself still in the innermost chambers of the palace. He has not yet well begun. But even if he reached the stairs, the courts would have to be crossed, and after the courts a second outer palace, and more stairs and more courts, and so on for thousands of years. No one could fight his way through all of this. All you can do, says Kafka, is sit at your window when evening falls and dream of a messenger who never comes.

But for all who are sitting by their windows and for all who are in the busy marketplace, there is incredible good news. After thousands of years the messenger has come. The message has arrived from the king. It is a message of life-and-death importance, because it is a message about the ultimate meaning of life and death. Even more incredible, it has been brought by a Messenger whose life is the incarnation of the message. Through this incarnation we have entered into the fullness of our human existence and have seen the true glory of God.

CHAPTER 5

Presence

GOD IS DEAD. He spoke to us and now is silent."
Those familiar with contemporary literature will
recognize this statement by Jean-Paul Sartre as a common
theme. We are told that we live in a "time of the death of God,"
a time when God no longer acts in human history. Man's "inevitable" drift toward atomic catastrophe or the unbelievable
godlessness of recent wars are often cited as evidence. There are
many who see no way to account for the "hopelessness" of the
human predicament apart from the death of God.

Elie Wiesel, a gifted Israeli journalist, is typical of those who
agree with Sartre. During his years in a concentration camp, he
was overwhelmed by the evidence of evil in his fellow prisoners
and in his surroundings. One day he was forced to watch the
hanging of a young boy by the Gestapo, a hanging that lasted
more than half an hour because the boy's body was so light.
As he strangled to death in indescribable agony, most of his
fellow prisoners stood in stunned silence. One man spoke for
them all as he cried out repeatedly: "Where is God now? Where
is God now?" Deep within his own life, Elie Wiesel was certain
of the answer. "God is there—on the gallows—dead." Though
many years have passed, he is still convinced that God is dead,
sharing this belief with countless others who have walked

73

through the valley of the shadow of death and found no sign of a living God.

In stark contrast to this "death of God" theme is the Christian conviction that God is alive. The certainty of this conviction is one of the most striking features of the Christian religion. Consider a group of completely demoralized disciples suddenly finding the power to carry the good news of Christ's coming to the whole Mediterranean world. Consider a church that has lasted nearly twenty centuries, always blossoming in new power just when it has been written off as dead. Consider the countless persons in every generation who have encountered a living God in prayer. Consider those who have been healed in mind and body by his presence. Today, as in the past, Christian life is not founded on concepts or ideas, but centers around continuing communion with a living God, who fills his people with "power from on high."

The God of Christian experience is not only alive; he is the Ground of life. He is the center and source of all created life, the living One who calls human beings into relationship with himself. This relationship, which we have emphasized as the key to human existence, is a continuing dynamic relationship between a conscious "I" and a living "Thou." The Christian reply to Sartre is that God is alive. He not only spoke, he speaks. And his continuous speaking is the source of hope for man and the world.

A. BEYOND BELIEF: GOD'S GRACE

From earliest times, Christians have been convinced that the "gift of the Holy Spirit" is a gift of God's grace comparable in significance to the gift of his Son in the incarnation. In fact, the two gifts were so inseparably related in the life of the early Christians that when they wanted to describe the living presence of God, they spoke of the Holy Spirit, the Spirit of God, the Spirit of Christ, or simply the Spirit. This inconsistency in terminology drove later theologians to distraction, but these early

Christians were simply trying to tell one another and the world about the grace of God, first manifest in Jesus Christ and now continuing as a living spiritual presence in their midst.

The second chapter of Acts tells the story of the Spirit's coming "with power" on the day of Pentecost. This "coming" was a sheer gift of God's grace, so overwhelming that the disciples struggled vainly to find words to describe it. They said the Holy Spirit came like a mighty rushing wind, but what did this mean? It meant that they had experienced God's presence as something so real and powerful they were at a loss to describe it. My own awareness of the difficulty they faced grew in an unexpected way during my first visit to Capernaum on the Sea of Galilee. As the leader of a study tour, I arrived fatigued and distracted, suffering from the intense heat, with spirits at a low ebb. The main goal of our visit was the ancient synagogue often visited by Jesus during his early ministry. Walking slowly through the ruins, I became aware of a quickening of mind and emotions, of an unexpected opening to the reality of God's presence. I noticed a narrow place in the shadow of the synagogue wall, so I sat for a time, reading Mark's description of the visits Jesus had made to this place. Suddenly I became aware of a cool wind blowing across my parched face, a wind blowing in from the sea, especially welcome because of the unbearable heat of a typical Galilean midsummer day. But there was more than coolness in the wind. There was healing and renewal as a sense of God's redeeming presence permeated my being. I sat for a time, letting myself be refreshed by this "wind of God," and for many days afterward I felt increasing gratitude for this experience of renewal at Capernaum on the shores of Galilee.

When pressed to explain the experience later, I found it impossible to describe in words. God was in the wind, but God wasn't the wind. God was in the traditions still evident in Capernaum, but God wasn't the traditions. God was in the words of Mark's Gospel as I read, but God wasn't the words. I tried to explain to one friend by saying that God was within me all the time, at the deepest center of my life, and the happenings of the afternoon simply made me aware of his presence. I could tell the answer did not satisfy him. Still, the presence was real and authentic to me, in some ways more real than that of the other persons who were with me at the time. But words fail to describe either the presence or what it meant to my life.

This incident helped me appreciate the difficulty faced by the New Testament writers when they tried to describe what had happened to them. I understand better now what they were trying to say when they spoke of God's presence as the rush of a mighty wind. I also understand why they spoke of this same experience in terms of fire. Pascal, the brilliant philosopher, wrote the one word "FIRE" while trying to communicate the nature of his greatest mystical moments with God. I understand what others mean when they speak of God as a light within or an inner voice, and what the Hebrews meant when they spoke of the Shekinah, the overwhelming presence of God in their midst. Those who have known God in this way use the most appropriate figures of speech, knowing that they have not touched the inner essence of the experience.

It is essential to note that the immediate result of the giving of the Holy Spirit at Pentecost was the creation of the church, the new community of God. Awareness of God's presence made the early disciples vividly aware of one another's presence and of what life together could mean. They began to share their lives (even their possessions!) at deeper levels than ever before. As a result of this life-sharing in the "fellowship of the Holy Spirit," they experienced a new power in their corporate and individual existence. There was a new depth of prayer, a new meaning to suffering, a new interpretation of marriage and family life, and a new appreciation for daily work. Anyone reading The Acts of the Apostles is struck by the amazing vitality and effectiveness of this small community of persons who had been empowered by the Holy Spirit. Never before in history had such a small group done so much. Even the enemies who cried out against them in rage were struck by the power of their life together. "They have turned the world upside down," it was said of them in amazement. If this was true, it was because God was with them, a living presence in their midst.

No one who has experienced the presence of God will doubt that he continues to "live" in the midst of his people today. We know that God is alive because we have encountered his living presence. We have been confronted by an Other, by One who calls us into communion with himself. Countless persons are as certain of the reality of this encounter with God as they are of the reality of their own existence. In fact, they discover the only reality to existence through this relationship with God. It is therefore absurd to speak of living in "a time of the death of God." Many persons may find themselves living in a time of the death of their awareness of God. But God is alive. He is the Ground of all of life. We speak with such confidence about our belief in the living God, because we have first known him in this living way.

B. Basic Belief

The publishers of a recent theological book built their advertising campaign around the question, What has become of the Holy Spirit? They were implying that the doctrine of the Holy Spirit has been neglected in contemporary Christian thought, but they should have pointed out that this is nothing new. In every generation there have been echoes of concern about the relative silence of theology on this vital subject. Long after the church had been at work clarifying its thinking about the doctrine of Christ, it had very little definite to say about the Holy Spirit. This "neglect" continues in our own day. The publisher's question is a relevant one. What has become of the Holy Spirit?

The New Testament writers would be astounded to find such

a question arising among Christians. In fact, the New Testament has been called "the book of the Holy Spirit." The term occurs nearly a hundred times, not counting the many references to the Holy Spirit as simply "the Spirit." This emphasis is even more striking when we consider how seldom the Holy Spirit is mentioned in the Old Testament. The Old Testament *ruach,* or breath, is often used to refer to the life-giving breath or power of God, but the term "Holy Spirit" occurs only three times. It is clear that some decisive event has taken place between the writing of the Old Testament and the New.

This decisive event, as we have seen, is the descent or gift of the Holy Spirit on the day of Pentecost (Acts, ch. 2). The life and work of Jesus Christ had prepared for this gift of the Spirit, indeed, the Spirit continued the work of Christ after his ascension. This means that the doctrine of the Holy Spirit is a distinctively Christian belief, though contemporary theologians are emphasizing that the Spirit has always been at work in the world. He has been and is present in the lives of non-Christians and all created things, but only those who have come into the life-giving relationship with God through Christ are truly *aware* of his presence. In this respect, Pentecost did not mark the coming of something new into the world, but the discovery by Christians of something already present. The real gift of God's grace is therefore the gift of awareness through which he sensitizes us to the reality of his living presence in our midst.

It is confusing at first to find personal and impersonal references to the Spirit in the New Testament, but careful examination reveals the purpose behind this practice. Ordinarily, when speaking of God as the Spirit, the writers use personal terms, but when reference is made to the power coming from God as Spirit, the terms used are impersonal. Thus "he" guides the disciples and tells them what to say, but "it" is received by the laying on of hands. Here again is evidence of the New Testament preoccupation with experiential testimony. The writers are not creating neat theological doctrines but witnessing to the life-changing reality of God's presence in their midst. Men and women, filled with joy and assurance of life, are performing wonders hitherto unknown and they wish to acknowledge that this new fullness of life is "of God." So they speak of being filled, empowered, guided, and led by the Holy Spirit.

Modern doctrinal statements are not nearly so helpful as this unsophisticated witness by the early church. One twentieth-century creed states, "We believe in the Holy Spirit as the Divine Presence in our lives, whereby we are kept in perpetual remembrance of the truth of Christ, and find strength and help in time of need." Another says, "We believe in the Holy Spirit, God present with us for guidance, for comfort, and for strength." These may be more theologically precise than any statement in the New Testament, but they are less effective in communicating truth about the reality of God's presence as the true heart of the matter. The most satisfying "doctrine" of the Holy Spirit will always be a person witnessing to the reality of God's presence in his life and to the difference this has made in every area of his existence.

The real theological stumbling block is the doctrine of the Trinity, because it involves the attempt to define the relationship of the Holy Spirit to the Father and the Son. The Trinitarian formula for describing God's essential nature is distinctively Christian and is one of the central "mysteries" of the faith. It is a mystery because there is no ultimately satisfying way of describing a God who is both one and three. The doctrine of the Trinity is a statement of essential monotheism, insisting on the one-ness of God, but declaring that his true nature cannot be expressed apart from an essential three-ness.

The concept is nowhere explicitly expressed in the New Testament, though some passages use a general Trinitarian form: "The grace of the Lord Jesus Christ and the love of God and the fellowship of the Holy Spirit be with you all" (II Cor. 13:14). Such statements are rare, however, indicating that the doctrine arose later, out of the church's life as it tried to explain the full meaning of the Christ event. Before Christ's coming, the disciples had known God as the Creator, graciously bringing men into existence and calling them into relationship with himself. When Christ came, they experienced this same God in a new way. He came to them as incarnate Redeemer, fully revealing the nature of the relationship with God intended for all men. After the ascension of Christ, they continued to experience God in this new way, but no longer through the incarnate body of their Lord. Hence, they spoke of God's presence as the Holy Spirit. In each case they are referring to the one true God, but since no single concept adequately expressed their experience, they began to use the Trinitarian formula. God confronts man as Father, Son, and Holy Spirit, but he is one God, the sole Ground of all being.

In attempting to define more precisely what is meant by the threefold oneness of God, the church has spoken of God "in three Persons," a practice that goes back to the third century. Translation of the Latin word *persona* as "person" can be misleading, however, because the third-century meaning is quite different from the meaning today. The word originally referred to the mask worn by actors in a play, then to the dramatic roles in the play, and only much later to the conscious self or ego, the individual "person." Use of the term today in connection with the Trinity implies that there are three personal divine beings in one God, a definite form of tritheism. In contrast to this, the doctrine of the Trinity is intended to affirm the threefold *oneness* of God.

For this reason, Karl Barth and other contemporary theologians persuasively argue that the attribute of personality should be applied only to God in his unity. In our communion with him we are confronted by one "Thou," one God who makes himself known in three ways of being. We have known this one God as the Father, gracious Creator and Sustainer of life. We have known him as the Son, manifesting himself to us redemptively in Jesus the Christ. We have known him as the Holy Spirit, the continuing living presence of himself within us, calling us to reconciliation with himself through Christ and empowering us to live in this fulfilling relationship. These three ways of being are not the work of three distinct "individuals," but of one God. Each is a true expression of his inner nature, of who he truly is. But Christians cannot say who he truly is in his fullness without referring to his creative power, his redemptive incarnation in Christ, and his continuing illumination as the Holy Spirit.

This way of describing the Trinity appeals to many persons as the most accurate way of stating Christian belief about the threefold oneness of God. In all fairness, however, it must be pointed out that a few contemporary theologians take a very different view of the matter. They are insisting that the phrase "God in three Persons" expresses an indispensable truth, the reality of communion or fellowship within the divine life. This view is often called a social analogy theory of the Trinity because it conceives of God after the analogy of social existence, though with a unity of fellowship exceeding anything known in human life. At first glance this view appears to be a form of tritheism, with God defined as a society or fellowship of deities. The more careful exponents of the position attempt to answer this criticism by insisting that each of the three divine Persons is not only a member of the society that is God, but is God himself. However, the inherent tendency of this view to slip into tritheism does not commend it to the modern age with its growing awareness of the unity of Ultimate Reality.

It is obvious that any doctrine of the Trinity only imperfectly reflects the inner mystery of the divine life. The essential thing is the degree to which the doctrine conveys something of the richness and fullness of God's revelation of himself through the coming of Christ. The Christian experience of God is so rich and meaningful that no one concept will adequately describe it. Contemplate the sheer wonder of a God who creates us for relationship with himself, who reveals the nature of the relationship in an incarnation of his own being, and who continues to come to us as a living presence deep within. This is the one true God as Christians have known him, God the Father, Son, and Holy Spirit.

C. BEYOND BELIEF: FULLNESS OF LIFE

We have emphasized that the experience of the Holy Spirit is a gift of God, an aspect of the divine life freely offered to all men. But only those who "receive" the gift through obedient discipleship become aware of the divine presence deep within their own lives. This is implied in the closing instructions that Jesus gave to his disciples:

Jesus said to them again, "Peace be with you. As the Father has sent me, even so I send you." And when he had said this, he breathed on them, and said to them, "Receive the Holy Spirit." (John 20:21–22.)

This indicates that the appropriation of the Holy Spirit will not be an automatic thing in our experience. On the contrary, there are at least two ways we exercise freedom in "receiving" the Spirit. First, we place ourselves in a position where the Spirit may become manifest to us. Second, we become increasingly attentive to God, eager to discover his will for our lives.

Placing ourselves in a position to receive the Spirit means primarily placing ourselves within the framework of the Christian community. The Holy Spirit brought the community into being, and through participation in the community individuals enter into "the fellowship of the Holy Spirit." It would be impossible to overemphasize the importance of this participation for those who wish to become aware of the Spirit. The community is the place where God has chosen to manifest himself in this particular way. I know of a banker who spends thirty minutes a day reading the Bible and praying alone in his office. He has nothing to do with the church because of weaknesses in the institutional life of a particular church he attended many years before. It is not surprising that he feels "something is missing" in his life in spite of his discipline of "daily devotions." Something is missing because he has chosen to position himself outside of the community where God manifests himself as the Holy Spirit.

This does not mean that the Holy Spirit is present only in the Christian community. It simply means that we become aware of the Spirit, sensitive to his presence, in this setting. God is redemptively present in the lives of all human beings, including those outside of the Christian community. He is present at every level of life in the natural world. It has even been suggested by Carl Jung and others that the natural drive toward health in psychiatric counseling is the work of the Holy Spirit. But even while agreeing that the Holy Spirit is present in every aspect of existence, we must insist that he is recognized as the Holy Spirit only by those within the Christian community. Within the community the individual receives the gift of awareness. He is sensitized to the workings of the Spirit around him and within him and he is given the power to accept the Spirit. Could this be part of the truth behind the often misunderstood statement, "Outside the church there is no salvation?"

This positioning of ourselves within the Christian community is the first thing necessary in receiving the Holy Spirit. The second thing is giving attention to God. This "giving attention to God" means earnestly directing our mind to God, giving heed to God, expecting God, waiting upon God, listening for God. It is true that God in his goodness often "arrests" our attention when we least expect him or when we are moving out of creative relationship with him. It is clear, however, that those who earnestly desire to live in the presence of God do not depend upon such experiences. Receiving the Holy Spirit according to the command of Jesus includes seeking, knocking, and asking in an attitude of readiness and receptivity.

Giving attention to God may take place in two principal ways. The first is what might be called *focused attention*. There are times when an individual deliberately seeks communion with God by adjusting all the phases of his life to the task of "waiting upon God." By an act of will, the intellect and emotions turn toward God and center or focus upon him.

Standing in Saint Jerome's cell beneath the Church of the Nativity in Bethlehem, I inquired about several egg-shaped objects I observed there, objects I had noticed in many churches in the Middle East. When told that they were intended to represent ostrich eggs, I naturally asked, "Why ostrich eggs in churches?" The guide explained that the mother ostrich lays her eggs in the sand and carefully covers the spot so that other animals cannot find them. She covers them so well, in fact, that if she looks away from the hiding place, she will lose them herself. She must therefore stand at rigid attention, staring straight at the spot, looking neither to the left nor to the right. No distraction, no temptation can cause her to look away, because her focused attention is a matter of life and death importance to her future offspring. Her example has been helpful to generations of Christians who need to be reminded to look straight at God during the period of worship. No outside noise, no inner temptation, should distract the worshiper as he "stares" at God. Similarly, certain regular periods of time during the week call for this kind of focused attention.

It is striking to note how often Jesus went off by himself to pray in this way. These notices are even more impressive when we remember that the Gospels were not written to record the inner consciousness of Jesus so much as to communicate what he meant to his followers. The fact that so many references appear in these records indicates that this was a common practice in his life. Some people are able to build several periods of prayer into their normal daily schedule; others find it difficult to maintain any regularity at all in this phase of their existence, but the

example of Jesus indicates that some definite times of concentrated attention are essential to every life.

Regular periods of prayer are not the only opportunity for
focused attention, however. Unexpected experiences of suffering
often lead us to seek a deeper relationship with God in very
direct ways. This deeper relationship may result in the healing
of mind and body and in relief from the suffering. One of the
most encouraging signs of renewal in the life of the contemporary
church is the rediscovery of the New Testament practice of healing by concentrated attention upon God's healing presence in
our individual and corporate lives. Even where physical healing
does not occur, there may be a healing at deeper levels as the
individual experiences greater wholeness of life and discovers the
redemptive possibilities in his suffering. The so-called problem
of suffering has plagued men from earliest times. How can a
loving God allow men to suffer? As long as we ask only the
intellectual question, the basic problem will remain unsolved.
The real question, the existential question, is asked by the Christian as he focuses attention upon God: "What creative growth
does God intend for me in the midst of this suffering?" The
Christian approach to suffering is grounded in the conviction that
creative possibilities are present in every experience of suffering
without exception and are revealed to those who seek God in
trustful attention.

The importance of these periods of focused attention is obvious.
Even those who do not look upon themselves as the "praying
type" often admit that they ought to pray more. What such persons fail to realize is that there is a way of "praying more" that
does not involve large segments of time taken from other things.
This might be called the way of *conditioned attention* to God.
By conditioning ourselves to be open to God at all times we
soon discover that many of the most creative moments of
communion come when we are outwardly most distracted. The
one thing needful comes to us in the midst of our concern over

many things, or it may come in and through the most common experiences of our daily existence. When we are aware of God as the Ground of our being we enter into creative encounter with him in every area of being. This means that we not only find God by retreating from the world to him. It means that we also find God by letting him penetrate through the world to us.

I discovered something of what this means when our second child was born. We were joyful at the coming of another child, but I inwardly groaned at the thought of the 2:00 A.M. feedings— stumbling in the dark, heating the formula, trying to stay awake during the interminable minutes it took the baby to finish the bottle. But one night my whole attitude toward this parental duty was transformed. I had been reading a book on the monastic life and was impressed by the way the monks in many religious orders arise at 2:00 A.M. to begin their daily prayers. Here I was awake at the same time, but miserably eager to get back to bed. Suddenly I quieted down and was amazed to discover the number of things we can pray about at 2:00 A.M.! The wonder of a newborn baby, the healing silence of the night, the people I knew who were lonely or in pain, the mystery of love—these and many other things crowded into my mind as I became intensely aware of God's presence in the middle of the night.

But if in a 2:00 A.M. feeding, why not in countless other common things? Why not in lifting a telephone, visiting a friend, cutting the grass, reading the paper, eating, dressing, sleeping? And if in these things, why not in daily work and marriage and leisure time? By conditioning ourselves to be open to God in every area of life we discover that he comes to us more often in the common things than in the uncommon, more often in the daily round than in periods of mystical ecstasy. I have visited the Holy Land several times, and I always come away with vivid memories of the common things I have seen: rocks, trees, springs of water, animals, children, mothers, bread, fire, wind, sun, and rain. And always I feel deepening gratitude for the way the

Christ event makes possible the finding of God in such common things as these.

This emphasis is in no way intended to discourage the practice of focused attention upon God during periods of time set aside for prayer. Such periods are necessary. But those who find themselves caught up in a busy and productive life also need to learn that we can condition ourselves to be aware of God every moment. This will take a great deal of conscious effort at first, but as patterns of attention are established we will find it increasingly less difficult to pray "without ceasing." Such a life is exciting, because we never know what new gift of grace awaits us around the next corner, and it is creatively secure because it is continuously grounded in God.

We have now seen how positioning ourselves in the community of faith and giving attention to God enable us to receive the Holy Spirit. Those who receive the Spirit in this way know why the early Christians wrote with such joy about this divine gift. Joy is the only possible reaction to the discovery that God, the Ground of all being, is vitally and eternally seeking communion with all men and with each one of us individually. Søren Kierkegaard once suggested the worst thing that could happen to a person would be to find himself roaming the earth, rejected and utterly alone, lost in meaningless wandering. But such a predicament is inconceivable to those who have received the Holy Spirit. We know that we can never be utterly alone, for at the center of our being there is a living God, eternally seeking to bring us into a relationship with himself that forever banishes our loneliness and our despair.

CHAPTER 6

Community

"THE MAN WHO LOVED ISLANDS" is the title of a haunting short story by the British writer, D. H. Lawrence. It is primarily about a man who longed for the solitude of life apart from others because he hated people. Using most of his savings, he purchased an island, hoping to find happiness in a life of total seclusion. He was always restless, however, never finding any lasting satisfaction, certain that the island was to blame. Though it involved a considerable financial loss, he sold the first island and moved to another, then to another and another. He spent the rest of his life moving from island to island, looking for solitary happiness until he became hopelessly insane.

It may be that the reason for so much of the insanity of our time is found in our own love of islands. As human beings we have been created for life together, but we continually attempt to live in isolation. We are in daily contact with many people, but creatively related to very few. We live in families, but even here we do not know how to share our lives at the deepest levels. We participate in the programs and activities of many organizations, but never become deeply involved as persons. What is most tragic of all, many of us attend some form of the organized church without ever knowing the unparalleled joy of participation in "the fellowship of the Holy Spirit." Restless and anxiety-ridden, we look for peace by moving from one island to another, never realizing that meaningful existence is realized only in creative life-sharing with others.

A. Beyond Belief: God's Grace

Opportunity for life-sharing fellowship with other Christians is one of the richest gifts of God's grace. The experience is unlike anything we have learned to expect from our usual associations with others, because Christian community is grounded in the love of God for his people. It is not something we create or bring into being, but a fellowship into which we are drawn through our life in Christ. In this redemptive fellowship called into being by God we discover for the first time what it really means to be loved and to love. We have been emphasizing the relationship with God revealed by Christ (reconciliation) as the key to human existence. In essence it is a relationship between the individual and God, but to our amazement we discover that as we enter into this relationship with God we are at the same time drawn into creative association with others. We are literally born again into a new family, a new fellowship of sharing, a new community of love. This being born into community is not something we accomplish but something we receive.

Astonishment and joy are often written across the faces of those who have just come into this new community. In some cases we have been trying to live in isolation from others, like the man who loved islands. Others of us have been immersed in social activity, yet finding no lasting satisfaction in our superficial associations with others. Then, to our utter amazement, we discover the joy that life in the Christian community brings to isolated souls, to overactive people, to frustrated church members. Here is a place where rebellion is accepted and forgiven, where selfishness is conquered by love, where hidden guilt is brought into the light, where anxiety is examined and overcome. There is no way to describe this new life in the Christian community except to say that we begin to live in a new world. It is a world created by the Holy Spirit, in which life revolves around God's love for us and our love for God and man.

The most obvious thing about this Christian community at first is the new strength we receive from it. We often come in great need and find that our needs are met, like coming home at a time when we need to be fed and strengthened by our family. Here we find that we are accepted and forgiven and loved. We discover that we are understood even when we strike out at others in rebellion. We begin to confess our need and our weakness, realizing we can trust those around us. Self-pity and loneliness are overcome because we are held and supported by the continuing and dependable love of others. We are healed, nourished, and strengthened as our lives merge with others at the deepest levels of human existence. In our great need we hunger for this fellowship with an insistent craving that will not be denied.

Even more amazing than this strength we receive from the community is the discovery that we can give strength to others. Slowly, almost imperceptibly at first, we begin to turn outward and look beyond ourselves. Our own needs become less urgent, and the needs of others loom large in our thinking. We begin to love others as they have loved us. We love some even when they have not loved us. To our astonishment, for we never dreamed of this before, we actually want to love them, want to help them, want to sacrifice ourselves for them. Then, as we grow in love, we find ourselves moving with the community out into the world. We long to share with the world the amazing riches of life in Christ. We begin to understand what we never understood before, why men such as Bonhoeffer are willing to go forth from the community to die in order that others may begin to live. Before entering the Christian fellowship, such love was inconceivable to us, but now we find within ourselves the strength to love in this way.

The deeper we enter into this fellowship of life-sharing, the more we are certain it is a gift of sheer grace. There is nothing we have done, nothing we can do, to bring such a community into existence. We understand that it is the means God has provided to nourish us in our new life with him and the means he uses to call others to this life of creative fulfillment. The importance of this fact will become clear as we examine Christian belief about the church. There has been far too much conversation about the church based upon the assumption that it came into being and exists as a result of human initiative. Whatever else is said or done about the life of the church in the modern world, we need to remember that it is first of all a gift of God's grace, and not a human achievement.

B. Basic Belief

Up to this point in our discussion we have been emphasizing the *spiritual church,* the unique and powerful fellowship of sharing created by the Holy Spirit. Unfortunately, many persons fail to distinguish between this spiritual fellowship and the *institutional church,* the organized structure created by men for the perpetuation and extension of the fellowship. The two are closely related, and under ideal circumstances the institutional church faithfully expresses the life of the spiritual community. There is a natural tendency, however, for the institutional structure to harden and become an end in itself. When this happens, the organized church becomes weak and ineffective, intent upon saving its own life rather than losing its life for the sake of others. Under such circumstances it deserves the devastating criticism of friend and foe alike. Because such criticism is so common today, it is necessary to clarify very carefully the major points of Christian belief about the spiritual church and institutional church, especially the nature of their relationship to one another.

The nature of the spiritual church is helpfully revealed in the meaning of three Greek words used by New Testament writers to describe the Christian community. The most prominent word is *ekklēsia,* used more than fifty times in the New Testament, mostly in The Acts of the Apostles and the letters of Paul. It is translated "church" in our English versions of the Bible, but literally means "an assembly of persons," with emphasis upon the idea of their having been "called forth." This idea is an effective way of emphasizing that the church is a result of God's activity in human history. Out of all the people in the world, a few have been called forth by God to be together in this particular way.

Such an idea is deeply rooted in the Biblical tradition. One of the earliest and most persistent themes in the Old Testament is that of Israel as a "chosen" people. At the time of the exodus from Egypt and in the wilderness wandering, the Hebrews developed a self-conscious awareness of themselves as an especially chosen community. Out of all the people of the earth God had favored them with his protection and chosen them to be his people. They had been "no people" before the exodus, but now they were God's people.

Thus says the Lord God: On the day when I chose Israel, I swore to the seed of the house of Jacob, making myself known to them in the land of Egypt, I swore to them, saying, "I am the Lord your God." (Ezek. 20:5.)

This idea of God's choosing Israel may be found at nearly every point in the Old Testament story. The people of Israel had been called forth by God and molded into a community in order to play a particular role in history.

This same idea is carried over into the New Testament idea of the church. Other words could have been chosen to describe the Christian community, but *ekklēsia* best expressed the way the Christians felt about their life together. On Pentecost the followers of Jesus came to a self-conscious awareness of themselves as a unique community. Those who had been with Christ and had come to a new relationship with God through him now became conscious of their new relationship with one another. But this was not their own doing; it was a gift of God. They felt that they had been chosen or called forth by God to be his people in a unique way. The word *ekklēsia* therefore helps us understand that the church is a community created by God, a community made up of persons who have been "called forth" by him.

A second word used in the New Testament to describe the nature of life within the Christian community is *koinōnia* (cf. Acts 2:42). The word means "fellowship," but this English word fails to convey the richness of life-sharing intended by the New Testament writers. Part of the reason for this is our tendency to associate the word with many of the superficial activities of the organized church. We constantly hear about fellowship suppers, fellowship teas, fellowship programs, and fellowship committees. This is what led one man to say in despair: "My church is nothing but a hymn-singing Rotary Club. We fellowship each other to death."

The *koinōnia,* the fellowship created by the Holy Spirit, is entirely different from mere social gatherings or associations of people. It is a community of life-sharing at the deepest levels, a community whose life together is grounded in the redemptive love revealed by Jesus Christ. Members of the community are so vitally linked together that they call themselves the body of Christ. Each member performs his own particular function, but he needs the others in order to live. As Paul points out, the members of the body are so closely joined together that "if one member suffers, all suffer together; if one member is honored, all rejoice together" (I Cor. 12:26). There is ample evidence throughout the New Testament of the radiant joy felt by the early Christians as they entered into creative life-sharing in this "*koinōnia* of the Holy Spirit."

The richness of this life together is a never-ending source of amazement to those who are privileged to participate in it. The mere physical presence of other Christians, for example, is a source of incomparable strength to the believer. How often Paul wrote from his Roman prison, expressing a longing to see his

Christian friends and have them near. Physical proximity is not a necessity, however, nor similarity of background or race or economic status. Those who are living in the body of Christ find that ordinary barriers and divisions are swept away. "For by one Spirit we were all baptized into one body—Jews or Greeks, slaves or free—and all were made to drink of one Spirit." (I Cor. 12:13.)

A simple laboring man once traveled six hundred miles to see me because he had read about this *koinōnia* in one of my books. On the surface we had little in common. His formal education was so meager that he felt ill at ease visiting me on a university campus. He had spent most of his life in a small town in the Midwest. His hands were soiled with the honest labor of a lifetime. He could not use theological terms to discuss his experience, but he wanted to tell me about his discovery of *koinōnia* and what it meant to him. As he talked, I felt all the barriers crumble instantly and I knew that we were one in Christ. We shared insights with one another, and our spirits nourished one another in this common sharing of life. Then we lapsed into silence because words were no longer necessary. We simply sat for a short time, feeling the joy and strength of the moment. I have seen this man only a few times since, and we seldom exchange letters. Visits and letters are not necessary. I feel as close to him now as I did on that glorious winter afternoon when we first discovered our common life in the body of Christ.

This deep sharing of life on creative levels of experience is one of the experiences God provides for those whom he has called forth. It is no wonder the early Christians couldn't stop talking about it. But this is only one phase of life in the spiritual church. Equally exciting is the way in which the *koinōnia* inevitably looks beyond itself to the world beyond. We discover we have been called forth not only to love one another but primarily to love the world. An important New Testament word describing this phase of the church's life is *diakonia,* meaning "service or ministry." It refers to the church's life of service to others, to the fact that Christians are called primarily to be a servant people. We are called to minister to others, to love others, to heal others, to call others into the fellowship, to die for others when necessary. This service to others is not simply something the church *does,* but something the church *is.* As Brunner says, "The church lives by mission as a fire exists by burning." By its very nature and through its whole life the church is called by God to serve the world and to be on mission to the world.

The people of Israel found that they were also to be a serving people, but the discovery was long in coming. At first they viewed their "chosen people" status as a privilege, learning only with great difficulty that being chosen involved heavy responsibility. They were to be a "light to the Gentiles," a suffering people whose wounds would lead to the healing of the nations.

It did not take the early Christians as long to make this discovery because of the example of their Lord. His whole life from beginning to end had been a life of *diakonia.* He had come, he said, as one who serves. He had washed the feet of his disciples to emphasize this fact. He humbled himself, sacrificed himself, and gave himself as the Suffering Servant Messiah who had come to seek and to save the lost. It is not surprising, therefore, to find the Christian community coming early to an awareness of its responsibility to the world. The New Testament reflects this awareness on almost every page, especially in The Acts of the Apostles, an entire book devoted to the stirring account of the early church's mission to the world.

Looking back over history it becomes obvious that the church has been strongest and most effective in those periods when it has most completely lost its life for the sake of Christ and the gospel in the world. This is one reason why a man such as Bonhoeffer fires the imagination of the church and fills it with new hope. As a respected German citizen, he could have submitted to the Nazi tyranny or he could have remained safely in exile abroad. But he returned to his own people, witnessing faithfully through his ministry in an underground seminary and through his own death by hanging at the hands of the secret police. It is significant that when they came to take him to the gallows, the guards said, "Prisoner Bonhoeffer, come with us." Were these words also spoken to Paul, prisoner for Christ, as he was led to his death? The sacrificial death of a Paul in the first century or a Bonhoeffer in the twentieth calls the church away from preoccupation with its own life to its servant ministry in the world. This aspect of Christian life, the *diakonia,* is epitomized in Bonhoeffer's haunting words, "When Christ calls a man, he bids him come and die."

The *koinōnia,* the fellowship of life-sharing, and the *diakonia,* the ministry of service to the world, are the two main aspects of life in the *ekklēsia,* the church called forth by God through the Christ event. All these terms help describe the nature of the spiritual church. The institutional church, on the other hand, is the organized external structure necessary for the perpetuation and extension of the life of the spiritual church. According to the earliest records at our disposal, the early church began appointing officials, taking up offerings, and giving birth to many organizational structures for the purpose of stabilizing and expanding the life of the *ekklēsia* in the world. These structures provided for the vital functions of preaching the word, dispensing the sacraments, maintaining the integrity of the ministry, and instructing the young. It was obvious from the beginning that organizational structures were as important to the life of the church as a physical body to a human being.

Unfortunately, our earliest records also reveal that serious organizational problems and weaknesses have plagued us from the beginning. The body tended to break down all too easily. First Corinthians and the Acts are filled with "church problems," including a fight over the preacher and worry over the collection. Such problems have been present in every generation, including our own. We have already noted the searing criticism of the organized church prevalent in our time. Kierkgaard spoke for countless modern persons when he cried out in his *Attack on Christendom*: "What has become of preaching? It has become a form of escapist poetry. . . . What has become of theological training? The candidate starts out to seek first the Kingdom of God. But he soon discovers that the first thing he needs to seek is a parish and a salary. . . . What has become of Christian education? Parents and teachers babble foolishly about what a beautiful world it is. . . . What has become of the ministry? There is not one honest minister. . . . But Christ has given the judgment on all this!" Similar criticism may be heard today, everywhere backed up by persuasive statistical evidence. Seminary enrollment is low, church school attendance is dropping, church membership is failing to keep up with population growth, and positions in the mission field go begging. No wonder Toynbee is so certain that ours is a "post-Christian age."

In every similar period of history, God has acted to renew the church by "reforming" the organizational structures so that they reflect more faithfully the true life of the *ekklēsia*. Just when the church seems ready to die, apparently missing the point completely, the wind of the Spirit begins to blow, bringing new life and new hope. What could be more exciting than the mounting evidence of this renewal in the church of our time! A new era for the church has obviously begun. The signs are everywhere. Suburbanites are talking excitedly about conversion and the mission of the church. Lonely apartment dwellers are discovering the healing power of community. Disadvantaged persons are hearing the good news of God's redeeming love. Outgrown structures of church organization are breaking and being turned into new forms. Mature men are leaving lucrative positions to enter the ministry. "Hopeless" social problems are yielding to the pressures of prophetic protest. There is indeed new life in the church!

One of the most promising signs of renewal is the rediscovery of *koinōnia*. The so-called small-group movement has become a powerful leaven within the life of the organized church, bringing new life to the whole body. These groups are springing up everywhere and for a multitude of purposes—prayer groups, study groups, Bible groups, therapy groups, vocational groups, mission groups. Here, persons are discovering the true nature of life-sharing at the deepest levels, the wonders of Christian existence in a community of love.

I know a young man who failed miserably in his vocational enterprises and planned to commit suicide. Members of a small prayer group he had recently joined found out about his despair and came together to spend the night with him. Some of the men in the group had to report to work the next morning, but this did not prevent their all-night vigil. They prayed with him, talked with him, and sat in silence with him. Then, as he explained later, "About 3:00 A.M. I felt their strength coming into my own body. I knew the crisis was over. I literally felt their strength coming into my life, giving me new courage. It was the turning point of my life."

I know a young woman, the product of a broken home, who was trying to work through the serious psychological problem of feeling unloved. Her face is radiant now when she tries to tell how she felt when she became a member of a small group of Christians and first discovered what it means to be loved and to love. Another young woman had such pressure to excel placed upon her by her parents that she broke under the strain. Now she tells of her joy and relief at being part of a group where, even though she may fail, she can still feel accepted and supported by persons who understand. Another person who was involved in a critical automobile accident is now deeply grateful that it happened because of her discovery in the experience of the healing power of the Christian community. All of these are examples of the rediscovery of *koinōnia,* examples that could be multiplied endlessly to show how the renewal of the church is taking place in our time.

Equally exciting is the rediscovery of *diakonia,* the ministry of service to the world. Young clergymen and their wives are moving at great personal sacrifice into the "slums" of big cities, creating relevant new structures of service. Churches are sponsoring new and "unconventional" points of contact with the world, places where honest dialogue may take place. The Christian coffeehouse in downtown Washington and church-sponsored fine arts festivals are examples. In places like these I have met persons who were really "hearing" the gospel for the first time. In addition, laymen are talking eagerly now of the true *laos,* the church in the world. The realization that when they are at work during the week they *are* the church on mission has revolutionized their thinking about Christian vocation and Christian discipleship. Equally significant, many clergymen are reforming their entire concept of the ministry, now looking upon themselves as ministers to ministers, their chief function being to train the lay ministry for mission and service. In these and other ways the church is discovering its role as a servant people in the modern world.

Evidence from other directions indicates that the renewal of the church is now taking place, such as the theological revolution we have mentioned and the movement toward greater unity in Christendom. The latter is reflected in the new posture of the Roman Catholic Church and in the powerful ecumenical thrust of Protestantism. Equally encouraging is the earnestness with which many individuals are trying to find their proper place in church renewal. Should they remain with the old structures and work to renew them from within, or should they abandon the old structures completely and work to form new ones? There is no way of knowing what the end of all this will be, but it is exhilarating to witness the beginning of a new era in the life of the church. The Spirit of God is at work in the midst of his people, renewing and reforming the organizational structures in radical ways. This inescapable fact may prove to be the most promising horizon of hope in our frightened age.

C. Beyond Belief: Fullness of Life

Our individual decision about involvement in church renewal through participation in a local congregation is a matter of crucial significance. The degree of fullness and maturity in our life as Christians is often determined by this decision. It is not a matter of whether or not we participate in the church, but simply of how and where and when to participate most meaningfully. At least two questions confront us as we struggle with this problem.

The first is this: To what degree am I willing to become involved in the ongoing life of a local congregation? Let no one underestimate the importance of this question. A large amount of the weakness in the contemporary organized church may be attributed to the soft-sell tactics that have been standard procedure for years. In our eagerness to gain members, we have watered down requirements until the church has become the easiest organization in the community to join. What a contrast with the demands of Christ, who called upon his followers to give up everything! Deeply aware of this contrast, many local congregations are now requiring intensive preparation over a two- or three-year period before membership can be considered. Some are requiring the annual renewal of membership vows. A man who had joined one of these churches said his experience was similar to boarding a train. When he asked how much it would cost, he was told, "Your life." Then he said, "I became frightened at this and hid in the caboose. And I've been hiding there ever since." But it's better to ride in the caboose of a train that's headed toward home than in the engine of a train speeding toward an abyss. Church membership, rightly understood, demands everything of us, because it is a call to unconditional commitment, a call to leave everything and follow Christ.

Closely related to this is a second question that confronts every Christian: In which local congregation shall I become involved? This is not simply a matter of attending the nearest church, nor is it a matter of window-shopping and sermon-tasting. On the contrary, it is a matter of finding the congregation where we can gain the most and give the most. Every person needs a place where he can gain spiritual enrichment. We cannot live without it. We also need a place where we can give of ourselves to others. When our local congregation does not bring satisfaction in these areas, the tendency is to leave and find another. This may be the right course of action, but we need to ask ourselves two questions. First, is the fault in the church or in me? Often our own estrangement from God and our own unresolved conflicts are the cause of our restlessness in a particular church. Second, is God calling me to remain in this "weak" church and become an instrument for renewal? In our despair over church problems we may overlook the need for a ministry of sacrificial love in the very congregation of which we are a part. The decision to leave a particular church is not a matter to be taken lightly.

On the other hand, if we find ourselves constantly running into walls of opposition, if we feel ourselves growing bitter and cynical, it may be better to leave, at least for a time. Emil Brunner warned us about local churches remaining hard and inflexible, unwilling to be renewed. These, he said, will be passed over by God, who will find other means of offering reconciliation and healing fellowship to men. I remember waiting for a bus one night in the downtown area of a large city. A billboard on a large stone church caught my eye: "Revival Services Nightly! Come One! Come All!" I noticed that it was time for the service, but there was no activity, no sign of life. Curiosity led me to the open door, which revealed a minister shouting from the pulpit, an organist impatiently waiting for the service to end, and five people sitting in the congregation! I turned sadly to the crowds rushing by, feeling that this church was tragically out of tune with the music in the streets. Few things are more depressing than a dead church. If we find ourselves involved in one, we may have to leave. Leapfrogging from church to church is no answer, of course, but surely God does not expect us to drink from a dry well.

Our discussion of the church should end on a positive note, however. There has been enough negativism in the church in recent years. There has been enough scorching criticism. Perhaps the criticism was needed to startle us out of our lethargy. But it is more important now to be aware of the renewing power of God at work in the life of the contemporary church. As on the Day of Pentecost, the Holy Spirit is coming like a mighty wind and fire to shake us and to bring to us a new consciousness of our uniquely meaningful life together as his people. The reality of this divine power at work among us gives us new hope for the future and calls us to new responsibility.

The renewal of the church will be radical. Nothing less would be effective in a generation already wondering whether God is dead. It is now obvious that the power of the living God at work in his church will provide the answer to this wondering. This fact inevitably confronts us with several questions. Are we ready to be renewed radically? Are we ready to be broken and to venture out in unexplored areas of church organization? Do we realize how radical the renewal will be? Dietrich Bonhoeffer wrote from his prison cell to a godson about the church and said, "By the time you are grown up, the form of the church will have changed beyond recognition." Do we believe this? If not, then perhaps we have not yet been grasped by the power of the living God, who is acting to bring about the radical renewal and reform of the Christian community.

CHAPTER 7

Love

IN THE DAYS when Jesus of Nazareth was preaching in Galilee, the Romans were building magnificent temples a few miles north near the city of Baalbek on the steaming plains of Lebanon. Today, two thousand years later, the temples lie in ruins, memorials to a dead civilization and a dead religion. The ruins are so impressive, however, that as I walked through them for the first time I found myself comparing the religion of Jesus and the religion of Rome. Both tried to relate human persons to Ultimate Reality, but only the former succeeded in leading man beyond his egocentric predicament. Rome's failure in this respect is strikingly illustrated by the proximity of the three main temples at Baalbek.

A first-century pilgrim to these shrines began his visit in a colossal temple built in honor of the chief god of Roman mythology. Here he offered sacrifice, prayed, and paid homage to mighty Jupiter. His religious obligations fulfilled, he then hastened to the nearby temple of Bacchus, where he was given all the wine he could drink and all the sensual entertainment he could absorb. At this point the temple of Venus awaited him, offering elaborate rites designed to satisfy his aroused desires. His pilgrimage had taken him from acts of religious adoration to acts of erotic love.

103

The religion of Jesus also begins with adoration and ends with love, but the adoration is directed to a gracious God who is Lord of every area of existence, and the love that results is so radically different from erotic love that it defies comparison. The love that grows out of Christian experience is not erotic and egocentric, but selfless, redemptive, sacrificial, and universal. It is the only ultimately satisfying love, because it is grounded in the being of God himself. For this reason, it infuses all natural love, including erotic desire, with creative power and meaning. We call it Christian love, because it is most highly exemplified in the Christ, and we discover as it unfolds in our lives that it is one of the eternal wonders in the religion of Jesus.

A. BEYOND BELIEF: GOD'S GRACE

Christianity is *the* religion of love, a fact reflected by those who watched the young church in action and cried in amazement, "See how these Christians love one another!" They not only loved one another, however; they loved the world, loved it with so great a love that others said, "They have turned the world upside down!" Even today when someone is unusually selfless or benevolent, it is often said of him, "He is a real Christian." Selfless love is the preeminent trait of the Christian life.

A group of employees in a large business office once welcomed a new accountant by warning him about one fellow worker who wanted to be left alone. He had scorned every offer of friendship, they said, apparently hating everyone, including himself. But the new man rejected their advice and went out of his way to be friendly. Ignoring the initial rebuffs, he made a special effort to let the other man know that he cared about him. The other people in the office watched in amazement as this act of friendship helped a man who hated everyone gradually emerge from his shell and begin to relate to others. One morning shocking news came to the office. The friendly accountant had died of a heart attack during the night. When the

man he had befriended heard of it, he said with tears in his
eyes, "He was the only Christ I ever knew."

It is not surprising to find someone like this associating an act
of compassionate love with Christ and his followers. In the New
Testament it is perfectly obvious that faith in Christ results in
a new kind of life. Something actually happens to those who
become Christians. The focus of their lives shifts from self to
others. There is a new quality to their relationship with fellow
Christians and with those outside the church. It soon became
clear that Christianity was not only a way of thinking, but also
a way of living. It was not intended merely to tickle the ears
of the philosophers who were eager to hear something new, but
actually changed the hearts of men and set their lives in a new
direction. Christians in every generation have found themselves
loving others in a way they have never loved before, in a way
they never thought possible. From the beginning, this new kind
of love has been the most striking characteristic of the community of Christians.

The source of this new kind of love is God himself. Left to
our own resources, we could never love in this way. We could
never even imagine what Christian love is like because it does
not fall into the framework of human possibilities. But that
which man could never imagine or achieve on his own, God
has made possible through his own love for man revealed in
the Christ event. God in this way has opened up a whole new
world of love. John explains it simply and accurately by saying,
"We love, because he first loved us" (I John 4:19). The gift of
his own love for us is the gift that makes possible our new
creative relationship with others. Without this gift we would
never know about this kind of love. Even when men rejected
the Christ, God did not withdraw the gift, but turned the crucifixion into a triumph of sacrificial love. "By this we know
love, that he laid down his life for us." (I John 3:16.) "God
shows his love for us in that while we were yet sinners Christ

died for us." (Rom. 5:8.) Because God loves us, because he came to us in Christ, because Christ died for us, we love.

The ultimate source of Christian love is therefore not found in any belief about God, but in God himself and in his gracious gift of himself in Jesus Christ. This gift is an inevitable expression of his essential nature, because "God is love" (I John 4:8). God himself, the Ground of our being, is limitless, redemptive love, and it is our experience of this love which alone makes it possible for us to believe in love and to love.

B. Basic Belief

The fundamentals of Christian belief about the nature of Christian love may be summarized in two brief statements: (1) We believe that through Jesus Christ, God has revealed a new *kind* of love. (2) We believe that through Jesus Christ, God has revealed the possibility of a new *life* of love.

In connection with the first statement, a serious problem of communication arises. Strictly speaking, it is impossible to define the new kind of love revealed through Christ because there is no higher principle or category available for reference. Christian love is grounded in Ultimate Reality. It is an expression of the "fatherlike" nature of Being-itself. Thus it becomes the defining principle for all meaningful life, the criterion for all other forms of love, and the standard of evaluation for all human relationships. The problem is further complicated by the multiple meanings surrounding the English word "love." We use this one word to describe brotherly love, erotic love, filial love, marital love, and many other "loves." We even say, "I love chocolate!" Fortunately, the flexibility of the Greek language, with its several words for love, helps to establish the essential nature of Christian love. The Greek word used in the New Testament to designate the new kind of love revealed through Christ is *agapē* (pronounced ah-gáh-pay).

There are many ways of attempting to describe the essential

meaning of *agapē*. We may apply adjectives to it and say that it is selfless, redemptive, sacrificial, compassionate, universal, inclusive, empathic, creative, and Christlike. Or we may try to describe what *agapē* does, following Paul's example in his matchless hymn to love: "*Agapē* does not insist on its own way; it is not irritable or resentful; it does not rejoice at wrong, but rejoices in the right. *Agapē* bears all things, believes all things, hopes all things, endures all things." (I Cor. 13:5–7.)

Another way to highlight the uniqueness of *agapē* is to contrast it with other Greek words for love, especially *erōs,* the root of our English word "erotic." *Erōs* is basically egocentric, selfish love. Its expression depends upon the ego's needs, desires, satisfactions. It is a desiring love, a "wanting to have" love, saying to the loved person, "What can I get out of you to satisfy or please myself?" *Agapē,* in contrast, is a selfless love, a "wanting to give" love. It says to the loved person, "How can I give of myself to help you achieve the highest fulfillment for your life?" It does not reach out to grasp for self, but to sustain, support, heal, and redeem the other.

Erōs is the kind of love illustrated in the experience of a French underground leader who was in urgent need of a place to stay one night during the Nazi occupation of Paris. An elderly Jewish man offered to share his hotel room. Later in the night, the room clerk rushed in, awoke the Frenchman, and whispered: "The Gestapo are coming! But they are looking only for Jews. Pretend you are asleep and they will leave you alone." When the Gestapo broke into the room, they awoke the Jewish man and started to drag him away. Wild-eyed with terror, he grabbed at the Frenchman's leg, desperately pleading with him to help. "But I kicked him away. I remember," said the Frenchman, "pushing with my other foot until I broke his grip. I kicked him away and went on pretending I was asleep in order to save myself." This is the way *erōs* takes what it wants from others and then kicks them away in order to "save" the self.

Agapē, on the other hand, ministers to the needs of others and remains with them to the end. It is illustrated in Thomas Dooley, the young American doctor who worked tirelessly in a ministry of healing to the neglected poor of southeast Asia. Rising early in the morning to find them waiting, working without rest during the day, falling exhausted into bed at night, he burned out his life in compassion for others, agonizing over those he could not reach. I met him and talked with him at the National Press Club in Washington just six months before his death. Still in his early thirties, his body was riddled with a vicious form of cancer. He knew that he was dying. But he did not speak of his illness, nor of his pain, nor of his imminent death. He spoke only of his desire to get back to his jungle hospital and to the people who needed him there. No one could persuade him to let up during those last months. He worked in the ministry of healing until his body collapsed and until his strong hands were stilled by death.

This is an example of the new kind of love revealed by God through Jesus Christ. But isn't this actually an unattainable ideal, a counsel of perfection intended only for the few? On the contrary, the Christ event actually opens up the possibility of this kind of life for all men. It gives man the power to follow the way of *agapē.* It is, in fact, *the way* of life ultimately intended by Christ for all his followers, because it is the inevitable fruit of reconciliation between God and man.

We have emphasized that this reconciliation is the basic experience of the Christian faith and the key to the ultimate meaning of human existence. It is simply saying the same thing in another way to insist that reconciliation with God enables man to love himself and others in this new creative way. Christian life in essence is simply the moment-by-moment realization of *agapē* in our actual existence.

The power to love in this way is given to us by God. Natural man, man in estrangement from God, cannot love in this way.

He is still ultimately concerned about himself, and his love is inevitably a selfish love. Those who are reconciled to God, on the other hand, are ultimately concerned about God, a fact that has a transforming effect upon the self. We literally become new creatures, new beings, new persons. We enter into a new community and find ourselves in a unique relationship with others in the community. We look out at the world and see people "through new eyes." We find that we have actually been given the power to love in a way we never dreamed possible before we were reconciled to God through Christ.

This does not mean we suddenly become perfect. It simply means that we enter into a continuous process of growing in love, of moving toward perfection. Past generations of Christians have called this "sanctification," "being made holy." This being made holy means increasing and abounding in *agapē* by participation in the community of *agapē* and by expressing *agapē* to the world. The support of our fellow Christians is essential in this learning to love. We are nourished by their love and we are taught to love by responding to their needs. Then, together, we turn to the world and give ourselves in a ministry of love as Christ gave himself for us. Very early we discover that nothing else in life really matters in comparison with the *agapē* we receive from God and the *agape* we offer to others.

It is ironic that the contemporary church has had to learn so much about love from modern medical psychology. A well-established principle of therapy insists that a person cannot love others if he hates himself. Self-hatred is inseparable from hatred of others, even if we manage to put on a mask and disguise our true feelings. Thus, according to psychology, self-acceptance and self-affirmation are necessary if we are to enter into affirmative relationships with others. But this is what Christian faith has insisted from the beginning. It is not until an individual has a profound new awareness of his own self-potential through the experience of reconciliation that he is able to love others creatively. Reconciliation makes it possible for a person to accept himself as a child of God and to affirm life and freedom. This new appreciation for his own self then gives him a new appreciation for others and makes it possible for him to love redemptively.

This relationship is memorably illustrated in *Winter Light,* Ingmar Bergman's somber and icily beautiful story of an afternoon in the life of a Swedish pastor. As a Christian clergyman he knows that he is supposed to love other people, but he finds himself unable to help or love others because he fears that he is beyond the help or love of God. Such a theme is psychologically and theologically sound, and may be a conscious attempt to reflect the life of Søren Kierkegaard's father, who believed that he had committed the unpardonable sin. As a result, his relationships with other persons, including his own son, were disastrous. Christian faith insists that persons in this condition will be able to love others only when they have come to a new self-appreciation through an experience of God's love for them.

We have said that God has revealed a new kind of love through Jesus Christ and that he has given men the power to express this love in a new way of life. This new kind of love and this new life of love are the basis of Christian ethics. The central ethical concern of the Christian is simply how to express *agapē* in every moment of existence. His expressing *agapē* in turn becomes the primary means by which he witnesses to others and ultimately gives hope to the world.

During the Second World War, a man who claimed to be an agnostic was watching a group of persons about to be executed. A mother in the line refused to give up her baby, even when the guard beat her mercilessly. When the guard's back was turned, a young Christian woman pushed the mother out of line and quietly took her place. The agnostic, who knew the young woman, said, "If this is what Christian faith does, then I will be a Christian."

But this *is* what Christian faith does! It makes possible the expression of selfless love in concrete situations and in moment-by-moment existence. This revolutionary kind of love is the highest fulfillment of man's life, because it grows out of the deepest revelation of God's life. The most creative possibilities in our relationships with other persons are realized when we love with *agapē,* this redemptive love revealed and made available to us through Jesus Christ.

C. Beyond Belief: Fullness of Life

When Jesus was asked about the greatest commandment, the religious or ethical requirement most important for human existence, he replied with the command to love.

And one of the scribes came up and heard them disputing with one another, and seeing that he answered them well, asked him, "Which commandment is the first of all?" Jesus answered, "The first is, 'Hear, O Israel: The Lord our God, the Lord is one; and you shall love the Lord your God with all your heart, and with all your soul, and with all your mind, and with all your strength.' The second is this, 'You shall love your neighbor as yourself.' There is no other commandment greater than these." (Mark 12:28–31.)

For his answer, Jesus chose two commandments from Jewish law, one from Deuteronomy and one from Leviticus, but the way he combined them and the meaning he gave to the word "love" (*agapē*) turned them into something utterly new. There is even a deep paradox involved in the imperative form of Jesus' answer. *Agapē* cannot be commanded, because the power to love in this way is given to us only in response to God's love for us. On the other hand, it must be commanded because it is an absolute requirement of the Christian life and not something extra or optional.

When we begin to examine the answer that Jesus gave to the scribe's question, it does not surprise us to find the command to love God standing first. Everything else depends on this. The really striking thing here is the unconditional and all-embracing nature of the divine-human relationship demanded by Jesus. Every aspect of human existence is involved: heart (emotional), soul (volitional), mind (rational), and strength (physical). The Jewish law had not included the idea of loving God with the mind, but Jesus added this to the others to emphasize how we are to love God unconditionally with our whole being.

The command to love neighbor follows the command to love God. In the eyes of the world this love for neighbor is the most striking characteristic of the Christian life. It is radical and revolutionary in nature, universal in concern, and is not based upon an expectation of return or gain. Nor is it some vague love of humanity in general, but a love for specific individuals, difficult as this may be. One of Dostoevsky's characters complains: "I could never understand how one can love one's neighbors. It's just one's neighbors, to my mind, that one can't love!" But Christian love always includes those who are most difficult to love, even our enemies. Jesus told his followers that they must love and forgive those who despitefully used them and pray for those who persecuted them. Thus the whole life of the Christian is a movement of *agapē* toward others. François Mauriac tells about a priest who burned out his life in an ever-expanding ministry of love for others. During his last illness, he continually whispered the names of persons about whom he was deeply concerned. His last audible words summarized the nature of every authentic Christian life. As he died he said, "I shall never love enough!"

The command of Jesus includes love for God and love for neighbor. But does it include a command to love the self? This is one of the most controversial subjects in Christian thought. Many writers, following Augustine, insist that the command, "You shall love your neighbor as yourself," implies the command, "You shall love yourself." Others are convinced that it is a disastrous mistake to make self-love a basic matter of Christian obligation. Who is correct?

We may be certain that Jesus did not command his followers to love the self in an autonomous way. Autonomous self-love, love of the self that denies our total dependence upon God, leads to rebellion and estrangement from God. It is the main source of the tragic predicament of man. On the other hand, modern psychology has demonstrated the absolute necessity for self-love in terms of self-affirmation and self-acceptance. We have already seen how important this is for our relationship with other persons, but this is only part of the picture. Our whole psychological well-being depends upon our ability to accept ourselves and to affirm life, growth, joy, and freedom, but we can accept ourselves in this way only when we know that we are loved by God. God created us, God loves us, God offers us fullness of life. The methods used by traditional Christianity to denounce autonomous self-love have unfortunately caused many persons to hate themselves and reject themselves. The results of this kind of self-rejection are as disastrous as rebellious self-elevation. On the other hand, self-love as creative affirmation of the self under God is religiously sound and psychologically necessary. It is the kind of love of self implied in the command of Jesus, "You shall love your neighbor as yourself."

One important question remains. How can I achieve the highest affirmation of my own self under God? Jesus provided the answer to this in the form of a paradox. "Whoever would save his life will lose it; and whoever loses his life for my sake and the gospel's will save it." (Mark 8:35.) The first part of the statement quite clearly establishes the connection between seeking to save one's life and actually losing it. We cannot save our own life, we cannot achieve positive self-affirmation, by setting this as our goal. Concentrating upon our own self inevitably

leads to egocentricity and autonomous self-love. The direct intention of saving ourselves thus results in the loss of the self
through estrangement from the Ground of our being.

Some persons make the mistake of reading an immediate
connection into the second part of the saying also, but it does
not say that whoever loses his life will save it. Whoever loses
his life will *not* save it if he loses it *in order* to save it. The direct
connection breaks apart on the words "for my sake and the
gospel's." This means losing the self in God and concern for
neighbor, for these are the heart of Christ and the gospel. Concentrating upon God and upon God's will for our lives, seeking
to love our neighbor with *agapē,* we lose ourselves. But in this
kind of losing, there is the finding of true life, the life of creative
self-affirmation under God.

The Christian life thus begins and ends with God. It is not
ultimately a self-centered life but a God-centered life. Nor is
Christian ethics a humanistic ethics, an ethics invented by man.
It is a way of living rooted in the grace of God. It begins with
God's gift of grace in Jesus Christ through whom we discover
the deepest meaning of love possible in human life. It ends with
God's grace enabling us to live in a growing relationship of love
for him and others, a relationship ultimately leading to the
highest creative affirmation of true selfhood.

All of this was vividly illustrated to me on my first trip to the
Holy Land during the Christmas season. I was eagerly looking
forward to the observance of Christmas Eve in Bethlehem, but
to my dismay, we arrived in the shepherd's fields only to find
television cameras and crowds of people creating a babble of
tongues. This was certainly not what I had traveled halfway
around the world to find, so I wandered off into the night, seeking silence and solitude. All at once I became aware of hostile
figures lurking in the shadows. When I stopped, they began
circling me threateningly, and I remembered the words of our
guide, "Never let yourself be cut off from the group." How

strange that my search for Christmas peace in Bethlehem had brought me to this moment of fear!

Suddenly, one of the figures asked, "Do you know John Wayne?" Astonished, I replied that I did not know John Wayne. Then they all began to talk at once, explaining how Hollywood movies were so eagerly enjoyed by the children of Bethlehem, telling me about their schools and their families, sharing with me their dream of going to America. As they came closer, I saw that they were all young men eager to make friends with this tall stranger from a far country. I told them why I had come such a great distance to visit their city, and they nodded proudly. We talked for a long time in what turned out to be one of the most memorable experiences of my life. Finally, I told them I had to go back and rejoin my group. A little boy who had been tagging along with the older boys stepped forward. His tousled hair was as black as the night around us, and he looked at me with dark eyes sparkling with warmth and affection. I wondered if the boy Jesus might have looked like this child of the Bethlehem fields. Suddenly, he held out his hand and said, "Good-by, friend. I hope we will meet again."

Holding that small hand for a fleeting moment in the field of the shepherds on Christmas Eve, I experienced the meaning of Christmas and of incarnation at a deeper level than I had ever known before. This is what Christ's coming has made possible for all men—barriers of hostility and suspicion broken down, fear and anxiety overcome, and hands reaching out in a gesture of love. In just this way, the gift of God's grace in Jesus Christ breaks down the destructive barriers erected by human hatred and makes it possible for all men to reach out toward one another in love.

EPILOGUE

Christian Hope

THROUGHOUT OUR DISCUSSION we have been emphasizing the meaning of Christian faith for the present moment of existence. It is in the present moment that man's destiny is realized, not in some distant past or idealized future. Yet it is also true that the meaning of the present moment depends partly upon remembrance of the past and hope for the future. Christian faith turns into hope when it looks ahead and tries to determine what the fulfilling relationship with God means in terms of future existence.

What, for example, is the Christian hope about life after death? The mortality of all men is a given factor of our human situation. Every life will end in death. There are times when we may feel we will live forever, but sooner or later every man faces the inevitability of death. At the height of his career, Winston Churchill was walking in a garden with friends, joining in pleasant conversation. Suddenly, his glance fell on a dead sparrow beside the path. He stared at it thoughtfully for several moments, then walked away in silence. His friends said nothing, but noticed that tears had come to his eyes. The shadow of the inevitable end of all living things had been thrown across the great man's path. It is a shadow no man escapes. Even in the midst of life we are dying, and the end is coming soon.

116

Man finds it hard to accept this inevitability of death. One of his oldest beliefs is that something in him survives the destruction of the body. The ancient Greeks, for example, developed a sophisticated doctrine of immortality. The body, they held, is mortal, subject to decay after the moment of physical death, but the soul is indestructible by nature and continues after the death of the body in unending and eternal existence. Deathlessness is thus an inherent right of every man because of the natural "immortality" of the soul.

Contrary to widespread opinion, Christians do not believe in immortality. The term is often used in popular Christian thought as a convenient reference to life after death. But the classical idea of the natural immortality of the soul has no place in basic Christian belief. Christians, on the contrary, believe in resurrection. Man lives only by the favor of God whose Spirit within him is the source of his life. When God withdraws his Spirit, man dies. Nowhere in the Bible is the human soul regarded as naturally immortal. The only way man can live after death is by resurrection, by an act of God's grace in "raising him" to new life. When man separates himself from God, by rebellion against God, he cuts himself off from the source of life. In this way he dooms himself to perish and to return to nothingness. His only hope for continuing existence is resurrection from the dead through the power of God. Certainty about this resurrection is at the heart of Christian hope. The followers of Christ have already experienced the grace of God to such a degree that they are certain it will continue to sustain them beyond the moment of physical death. That which God has begun here on earth, the creation of finite beings capable of creative fellowship with him, will be continued and completed beyond this earthbound life. This continuation and completion will be made possible through resurrection by the power of God. The sign and seal of such resurrection is provided in the resurrection of Jesus Christ, an act of God that manifests God's victory over death to all men of faith. The fact that Jesus Christ was raised from the dead means that we, too, will be raised to newness of life with him.

Speculation about the future of the physical body often troubles modern Christians because we know that physical bodies are destroyed. Yet we repeat the Apostles' Creed and say, "We believe in the resurrection of the body." Those who take this phrase literally miss the central meaning intended by the early church. What they were saying is that we believe in the resurrection of the total person, not just some part of him called the soul. The whole person, soul and body, is raised to new life. But how can the body be raised? Paul faces this problem in one of the most significant passages in the Bible, the fifteenth chapter of First Corinthians. He begins with the observation that God has given every form of life here on earth an appropriate body. Plants, animals, persons, even the stars in the heavens have been properly embodied by God for life in a material universe. Those who have experienced the power and grace of God can therefore trust him to provide us with a proper "spiritual body" for the next life. When the physical body returns to the earth, God "clothes us" in a new body, appropriate for our continuing life of fellowship with him.

We have already suggested that the resurrection of Jesus is a convincing sign of God's gracious provision for our future. The resurrection of Jesus removes "the sting of death." A further sign of grace is found in our own daily experience of resurrection by the power of God. When Paul says to the Corinthians, "I die every day," every Christian knows what he means. We die a thousand little deaths every day as we struggle to overcome our rebellion against God. It is the disobedient, unloving, autonomous self that dies. But in every experience of "dying to self," I find that I am raised to new life by the grace of God. There is a literal resurrection of my dead, egocentric self to a new life of creative self-affirmation under God. This continuing daily resurrection by

the power of God makes it easier for me to understand and anticipate resurrection of the total self when my earthly life has run
its course.

But what is the use of all this speculation about the future
when we don't know how to live in the present? We need to
have this question raised by the critics of Christian faith because
we often miss the main point. One enemy of the church laughed
scornfully at Christians who worry about living forever when
they don't even know how to spend one hour meaningfully here
on earth. Emily's famous line in *Our Town* reflects the same
crucial problem: "Do any human beings ever realize life while
they live it every, every minute?" To which the stage manager
replies, "No." But if this is true, even of Christians, then our
attention needs to be directed to the reality and meaningfulness
of the present moment of existence. The real key to Christian
hope is found in the quality of life God provides now rather than
in some vague anticipation of an endless future.

This is precisely what is done for us in the Gospel of John,
where one of the dominant themes is "eternal life." Eternal life
is not mere endless duration but the quality of life provided for
us in each moment of existence by the grace of God in Christ.
This new dimension of life revealed through the coming of
Christ is not reserved for a time after death. It can be lived
"eternally" in the present. Living in this way is the purpose for
life at any given moment. It cannot, of course, be fully realized
here on earth. We look forward to its fulfillment after death. But
what we anticipate after death is not essentially different from
the highest realization of life available now through life in Christ.
What we are really saying is that eternal life is always present
and always future.

What is the essence of this eternal life available now? Jesus
defines it near the beginning of his long prayer in the upper
room: "And this is eternal life, that they know thee the only true
God, and Jesus Christ whom thou has sent" (John 17:3). This

is precisely *the essence* of Christian faith as we have been describing it. To know God fully, to enter into relationship with God, to acknowledge God as the Ground of our being, to accept reconciliation with God—this is what the Christian faith is all about. Now we discover that this same relationship with God provides the key to Christian hope about the future. Our chief concern is not about what kind of body we will have or what kind of "place" we will inhabit. Our chief concern is for relationship with God, knowing God fully. This is what provides ultimate meaning for our human lives, now and in the future.

There is a delightful story of an old woman who was seen walking through the streets of Strasbourg in the time of the great Christian mystic Meister Eckhart. She was carrying a torch in one hand and a pail of water in the other. When asked what she was about, she replied, "With the torch I will burn up heaven and with the water put out the fires of hell, so that in the future men will love the dear Lord God for himself and for himself alone, and not out of fear of hell or desire for reward in heaven." To love the Lord God for himself and for himself alone is the essence of Christian faith in each moment of existence, now and eternally.

But what about the future of the world? The death of individual persons is not the only cause of anxiety. The world is dying too. By this death of the world is meant the end of human history as we know it. Speculation about the end of history is called "eschatology," from a word that means "last things." The striking revival of eschatology in contemporary theology is largely due to our continuing international crisis. Many persons are convinced that the human race is headed for total self-destruction. A full-scale atomic war would be over in a matter of minutes with resulting desolation beyond the power of the human mind to comprehend. A mood of pessimism about the "impending end" has even permeated the Christian church. A prominent minister recently announced a passage of Scripture from the pulpit of the

Washington Cathedral. Then he said to the congregation, "I hope you will memorize this and keep it with you. You will find it comforting in five years when the darkness falls." He did not stop to explain what he meant. He did not need to. A healthy-minded Christian mother of three children said to me: "I don't believe my children will grow up in this world. The best thing I can do as a Christian mother is teach them how to die." We feel that such a statement is shocking, but we fear it may be realistic. It is no wonder that our present world crisis, pressing upon us the possibilities of imminent disaster, has led to a revival of interest in eschatology, the doctrine of the last things.

In a recent coffeehouse conversation, Christian belief about the end of history was the subject under discussion. Several persons were speaking despairingly about the potential world catastrophe. One man spoke up suddenly and said, "If a man is really a Christian, he doesn't care if the world blows up tomorrow." After long and heated debate, the group decided that this statement is very right and very wrong. It is wrong in implying that the Christian doesn't care about this world. He is involved in the world and has a burning sense of mission to the world. In many ways he cares more about the world than anyone else. But this statement is right in implying that the Christian is "not stuck with this world." God is greater than the world; God is greater than human history; God is greater than the worst evil that can befall the world because of man's sin. The Ground of all being will not be finally thwarted by man's rebellion, even the rebellion of the whole human race. In this sense, a Christian doesn't care if the world blows up tomorrow.

One reason this statement can be made with such conviction is the certainty of God's victory over evil. The reign of God has already come. God has broken the structure of evil in the world. He has demonstrated his sovereignty over the world and his victory over disobedience and rebellion. This conviction that God rules and that he has won the victory over evil makes a profound difference in a person's attitude toward the world in which he lives. Some of the military personnel who fought on the islands in the Pacific during the Second World War have told about the bloody skirmishes fought after the peace treaty had been signed. There was no way to get word to the isolated Japanese units that the war was over. They continued their desperate fight, and many Americans were killed. But those who came back described how different they felt when they learned that the peace treaty had been signed. Even though they had to continue fighting, it made all the difference in the world to know that the victory had been won. God turned the cross of Christ from apparent defeat into victory. He will do the same if man destroys the world. The fulfillment of God's ultimate purpose is assured, and "it doesn't matter what happens to the world." In this sense, the reign of God has already come and the Christian lives in the joy of victory won.

In another sense, however, the Kingdom of God is yet to come. It is not a contradiction to say that the Kingdom has come and is yet to come. That which has come is the assurance of victory, the foretaste of what God will do at the "end time." For just as history has a beginning (creation) and a center (Christ), so it has an end or final fulfillment. The meaning of history is given at the center, but the end is yet to be realized. For this reason the Christian labors in the world, prays over the world, agonizes over the world, and willingly dies as a part of God's mission to the world. He knows that the beginning, center, and end of history are under the rule of God. He knows that the end, like the beginning and the center, will come through the power of God. But he also believes that God is working through the Christian community to give decisive meaning to the present and to prepare for the end. How the Kingdom will ultimately come, how the fulfillment of God's purpose for history will be realized, is beyond our knowing. We may speculate about such things in our doctrine of eschatology. But the important thing is that the Kingdom *has come* in Jesus Christ, demonstrating God's sovereign power and purpose for all history, and is *yet to come* at God's good pleasure and in the fullness of time. This explains the Christian's abiding faith in the midst of catastrophe and his burning enthusiasm as he goes on mission to the world.

During the Second World War, a young Dutch patriot wrote to his family from a prison cell. He was to be executed the next morning. His words reveal his quiet courage, his lack of hatred, and his awareness of God's presence in those last hours. The letter, hailed as one of the most significant documents of the war, concludes with these words: "God rules everything."

These are the last words of every Christian life. In them we find the deepest meaning for our individual existence and our only hope for the future of the world. We know that nothing can separate us from the love of God in Jesus Christ because God rules everything. We know that our own existence can be meaningful and that society can be redeemed because God rules everything. Because of his rule we live and we shall live, beyond death and beyond the death of the world. And though our Christian belief concerning these things is of utmost importance, we must never forget that the ultimate ground of our hope is found beyond belief, in the continuing action of God's grace in our midst and in human history.

INDEX